Office 365 Microsoft Teams

Teams is an **Office 365 App** designed to improve visibility of information by consolidating it all into specific topics (**Channels**) similar to a project plan and tasks. Once defined, all information is placed in one location which will help you understand everything you need to know about a **Project**. Each **Project Team** will define groups of people to work together and view information in order to communicate with everyone on the **Team**. **Project Teams** can offer multiple **Channels** or subtasks to provide information on a focused objective. This centralized information, collected in a specific **Channel** (subtask), will be valuable for an existing **Team** as well as **New Members**.

This **Step-By-Step Workbook** will teach you how to create a **Project Team**, **Channels** (or subtasks), create a **Chat** environment to ask/respond to questions, store **Project** documentation, schedule meetings, evoke **Video Meetings** with the **Team** (similar to **Skype**), **Record Video Meetings**, store meeting notes to the **Channel**(subtasks), **Chat** with anyone in the enterprise (company), build **Teamsite (Team Website)**, consolidate all communications on one centralized location, and make internet phone calls from your computer!

When **Teams** is not used information becomes disjointed because it is stored in different **Email** folders and **Shared** server folders throughout a company. Also, the downside of *not* using **Teams** is that everyone on the **Project Team** will receive different bits of information, status reports, and different levels of **Project** updates. In other words, communication information would be scattered, not stored in one place, and new **Team Members** will have a harder time getting up to speed. **Microsoft Teams** is designed to improve the visibility of information and allow increased collaboration of ideas.

Another major concept covered in this manual is a **Teamsite.** This is a **Sharepoint Site** that contains a resource pool of information for a department, **Project Team**, resource pool, book club, or just general use. A **Teamsite** can be created from each **Microsoft Team Project** and can contain a **Central Team Calendar**, **Blog**, **Documentation**, **Text Page** (to explain a process), **Task List,** or whatever you wish to post for the **Team**. This **Teamsite** will provide information for the **Project Team** and others that are not defined as **Team Members**. This manual will specifically cover the basics of how to develop a **Teamsite** but is not intended to go into **Sharepoint** development.

Copyright and Release Information

Exercise Download

Exercises are posted on the website and can be downloaded to your computer.
Please do the following:

Open Internet Explorer/Edge: Or Google Chrome:

Type the web address: **elearnlogic.com/download/teams365-1.exe**

You might get several security warnings, but answer yes and run through each one. When you click "**Unzip**," the files will be located in **C:\Data\Teams365-1** folder.

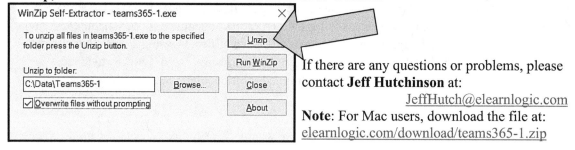

If there are any questions or problems, please contact **Jeff Hutchinson** at:

JeffHutch@elearnlogic.com

Note: For Mac users, download the file at: elearnlogic.com/download/teams365-1.zip

Obtain Your PDF and Recorded Video Course

To obtain a **PDF** copy of the courseware and a link to an **Online Recorded Video Course**, send an email to jeffhutch@elearnlogic.com along with your receipt/confirmation email from Amazon. Also, we provide **Remote Online** classes accessible worldwide in a variety of topics at: **www.elearnlogic.com**.

Table Of Contents

About the Author

Jeff Hutchinson is a computer instructor teaching a variety of classes around the country. He has a BS degree from BYU in Computer-Aided Engineering and has worked in the Information Technology field supporting and maintaining computers for many years. He also previously owned a computer training and consulting firm in San Francisco, California. After selling his business in 2001, he has continued to work as an independent computer instructor around the country. **Jeff Hutchinson** lives in Utah and also provides training for Utah Valley University Community Education system, offering valuable computer skills for the general knowledge of students, career development, and career advancement. Understanding the technology and the needs of students has been the basis for developing this material. **Jeff Hutchinson** can be contacted at JeffHutch@elearnlogic.com or **(801) 376-6687.**

Workbook Design

This workbook is designed in conjunction with an **Online-Instructor-Led course** (for more information see: **www.elearnlogic.com**). Unlike other manuals, you will not need to review lengthy procedures to learn a topic. All that is needed are the brief statements and command paths located within the manual that demonstrate how a concept is used. Furthermore, you will find that this **Workbook** is often used as a reference to help understand concepts quickly, and an index is provided on the last page to reference pages as necessary. However, if more detail is needed, you can always use the Internet to search for a concept. Also, if your skills are weak due to lack of use, you can refresh your memory quickly by visually scanning the concepts needed and then testing them out using the application.

Manual Organization

The following are special formatting conventions:

- **Numbered Sections** on the left are the **Concepts** covered.
- **Italic Text** is a Step-By-Step procedure to better understand a concept.
- **Practice Exercises** are a **Step-by-Step** approach to demonstrate the **Concept**.
- **Student Projects** are a more comprehensive approach to demonstrate the **Concept**.
- **Dark, Grayed-Out Sections** are optional/advanced **Concepts**.
- **Bolded** items are important points, terminology, or commands.
- **Tips** are additional ideas to help better understand the **Concept**.

Chapter 1 - Create a Team and Channels

The first step in the process is to create a **Team** and **Channel**. The **Team** will focus on a specific topic or main subject, and the **Channels** will be subtopics or actions that need to be performed. Once you set up **Team** and **Channels**, **Members** of the **Team** can be added and participate by providing valuable content towards the **Team** goals.

Chapter Contents:

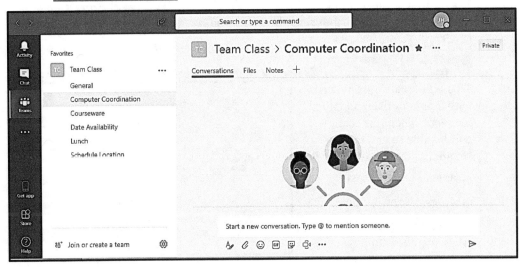

Section 1 - Teams

The **Teams Button** is the primary hierarchical element in this program. Everything under the **Team** name will provide information gathered for that **Team Project**. In this section, we will focus on setting up the **Team** to be used. See **Microsoft's** website at: **https://teams.microsoft.com** for more information.

Concept	Explanation / *Command String in italic*.
1.1 Teams Office 365 App	First, log in to **Office 365** and you will see the **Teams** web-based **App** available if you are using the **Business Version of Office 365**. The web-based **App** will not provide all the features, but it will allow for **Team** and **Channel Conversations**. Apps: Outlook, OneDrive, Word, Excel, PowerPoint, OneNote, SharePoint, Teams
1.2 Teams Desktop App	The **Teams Desktop** application is installed on your desktop which will provide more functionality and quicker response times using **Video** and **Audio Meetings**. It is recommended that you use the **Teams Desktop** application in conjunction with this workbook. Microsoft **Teams** Desktop app **Microsoft Teams Download**: https://teams.microsoft.com/download

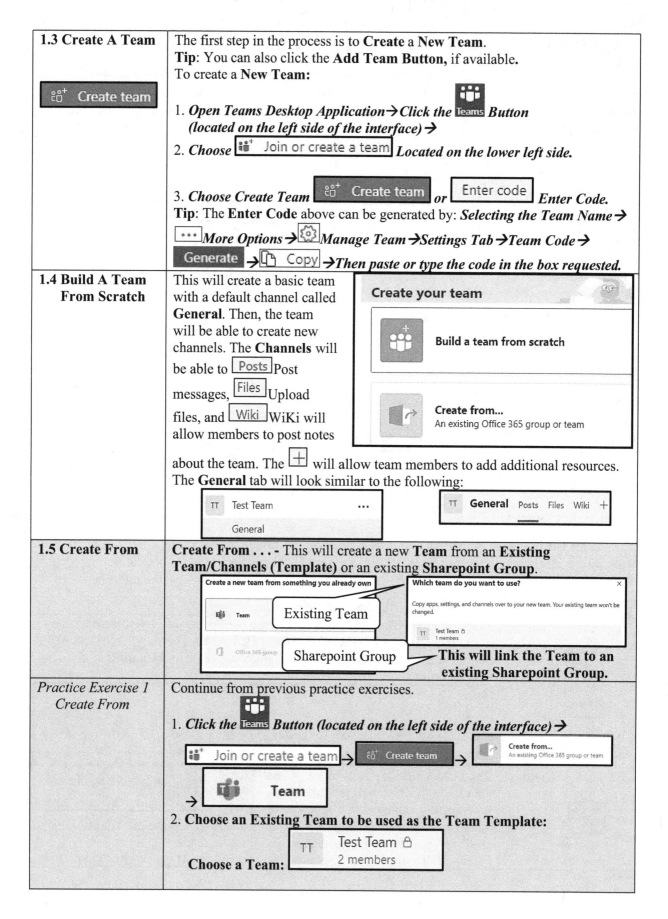

1.3 Create A Team ⊞ Create team	The first step in the process is to **Create a New Team**. **Tip**: You can also click the **Add Team Button,** if available. To create a **New Team:** 1. ***Open Teams Desktop Application→Click the*** Teams ***Button (located on the left side of the interface)→*** 2. ***Choose*** Join or create a team ***Located on the lower left side.*** 3. ***Choose Create Team*** Create team *or* Enter code ***Enter Code.*** **Tip**: The **Enter Code** above can be generated by: ***Selecting the Team Name→*** ⋯***More Options→***⚙***Manage Team→Settings Tab→Team Code→*** Generate →⧉ Copy →***Then paste or type the code in the box requested.***
1.4 Build A Team From Scratch	This will create a basic team with a default channel called **General**. Then, the team will be able to create new channels. The **Channels** will be able to Posts Post messages, Files Upload files, and Wiki WiKi will allow members to post notes about the team. The ⊞ will allow team members to add additional resources. The **General** tab will look similar to the following: **Create your team** Build a team from scratch **Create from...** An existing Office 365 group or team TT Test Team ⋯ / General TT **General** Posts Files Wiki +
1.5 Create From	Create From . . . - This will create a new **Team** from an **Existing Team/Channels (Template)** or an existing **Sharepoint Group**. Create a new team from something you already own — Existing Team Team Office 365 group — Sharepoint Group Which team do you want to use? ✕ Copy apps, settings, and channels over to your new team. Your existing team won't be changed. TT Test Team 🔒 / 1 members **This will link the Team to an existing Sharepoint Group.**
Practice Exercise 1 Create From	Continue from previous practice exercises. 1. ***Click the*** Teams ***Button (located on the left side of the interface)→*** Join or create a team → Create team → Create from... An existing Office 365 group or team → Team 2. **Choose an Existing Team to be used as the Team Template:** TT Test Team 🔒 / 2 members **Choose a Team:**

	3. *Enter the Team Name and select the options below:* **Team Name:** *Team Template (initials).* **Tip:** Place your initials in the name if there are multiple students in the class. 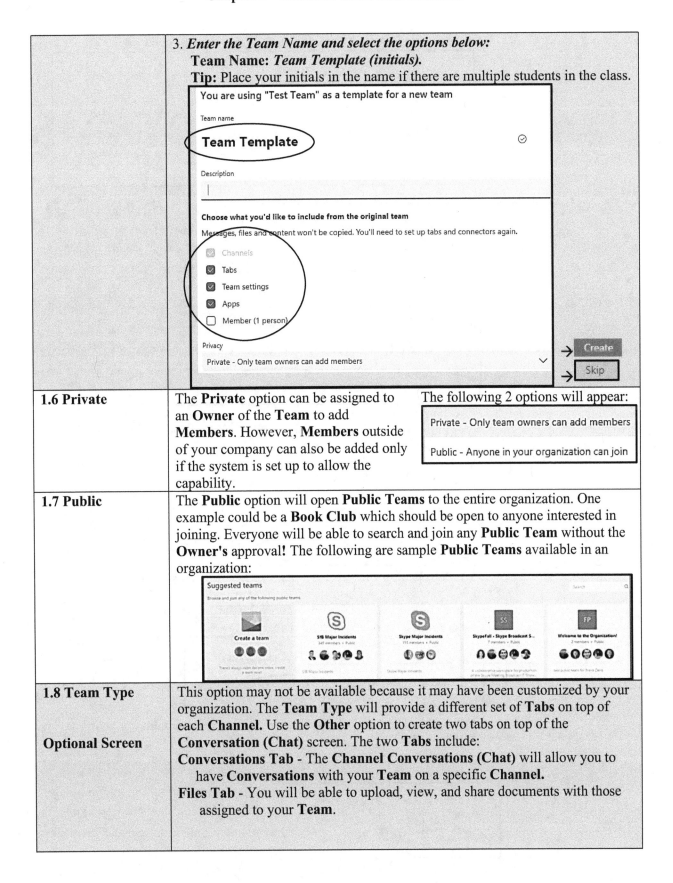
1.6 Private	The **Private** option can be assigned to an **Owner** of the **Team** to add **Members**. However, **Members** outside of your company can also be added only if the system is set up to allow the capability. The following 2 options will appear: Private - Only team owners can add members Public - Anyone in your organization can join
1.7 Public	The **Public** option will open **Public Teams** to the entire organization. One example could be a **Book Club** which should be open to anyone interested in joining. Everyone will be able to search and join any **Public Team** without the **Owner's** approval! The following are sample **Public Teams** available in an organization:
1.8 Team Type **Optional Screen**	This option may not be available because it may have been customized by your organization. The **Team Type** will provide a different set of **Tabs** on top of each **Channel**. Use the **Other** option to create two tabs on top of the **Conversation (Chat)** screen. The two **Tabs** include: **Conversations Tab** - The **Channel Conversations (Chat)** will allow you to have **Conversations** with your **Team** on a specific **Channel**. **Files Tab** - You will be able to upload, view, and share documents with those assigned to your **Team**.

When you create a **New Team**, you will receive the following:

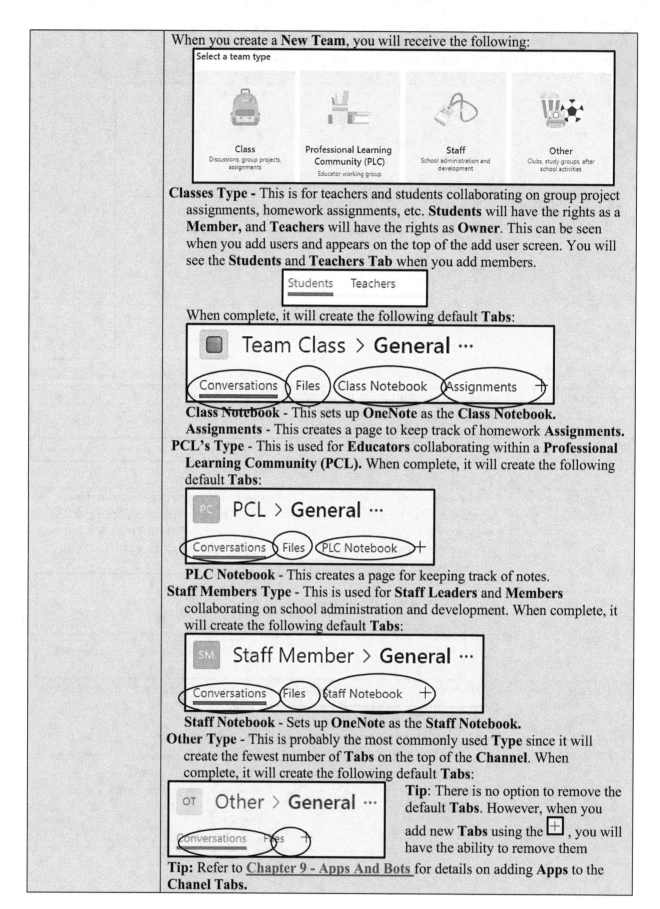

Classes Type - This is for teachers and students collaborating on group project assignments, homework assignments, etc. **Students** will have the rights as a **Member,** and **Teachers** will have the rights as **Owner**. This can be seen when you add users and appears on the top of the add user screen. You will see the **Students** and **Teachers Tab** when you add members.

When complete, it will create the following default **Tabs:**

Class Notebook - This sets up **OneNote** as the **Class Notebook.**
Assignments - This creates a page to keep track of homework **Assignments.**
PCL's Type - This is used for **Educators** collaborating within a **Professional Learning Community (PCL).** When complete, it will create the following default **Tabs:**

PLC Notebook - This creates a page for keeping track of notes.
Staff Members Type - This is used for **Staff Leaders** and **Members** collaborating on school administration and development. When complete, it will create the following default **Tabs:**

Staff Notebook - Sets up **OneNote** as the **Staff Notebook.**
Other Type - This is probably the most commonly used **Type** since it will create the fewest number of **Tabs** on the top of the **Channel**. When complete, it will create the following default **Tabs:**

Tip: There is no option to remove the default **Tabs**. However, when you add new **Tabs** using the ⊞ , you will have the ability to remove them

Tip: Refer to <u>Chapter 9 - Apps And Bots</u> for details on adding **Apps** to the **Chanel Tabs.**

Chapter 1 - Create A Team And Channels

Practice Exercise 2 *Display Public* *Teams*	To see a list of all **Public Teams** available: 1. ***Open Microsoft Teams Desktop application→*** ***Go to the command search box at the top of Teams→Type: /join*** 2. If you receive the following message, then **Public Teams** is not available: 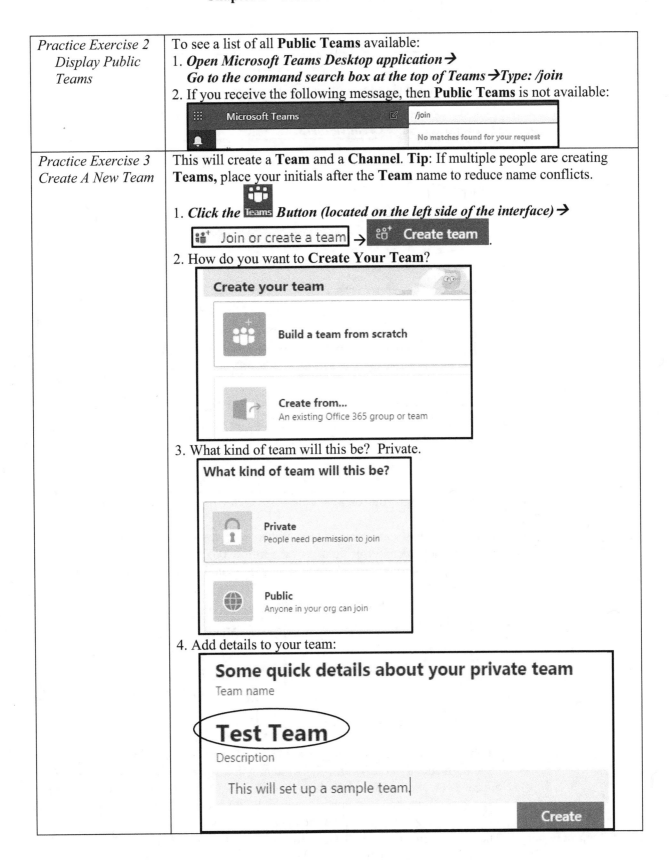
Practice Exercise 3 *Create A New Team*	This will create a **Team** and a **Channel**. **Tip**: If multiple people are creating **Teams,** place your initials after the **Team** name to reduce name conflicts. 1. ***Click the*** Teams ***Button (located on the left side of the interface) →*** [⬚⁺ Join or create a team] → [⬚⁺ Create team] . 2. How do you want to **Create Your Team**? **Create your team** [Build a team from scratch] [Create from... An existing Office 365 group or team] 3. What kind of team will this be? Private. **What kind of team will this be?** [🔒 Private People need permission to join] [🌐 Public Anyone in your org can join] 4. Add details to your team: **Some quick details about your private team** Team name **Test Team** Description This will set up a sample team. [Create]

	5. Add **Members** to the new **Team**. **Add members to Test Team** → Skip 6. Add a **Channel** to test out the new **Team**. *Team Name* → ··· *More options* → 📧 *Add Channel* → **Channel Name:** *Creative Ideas*. 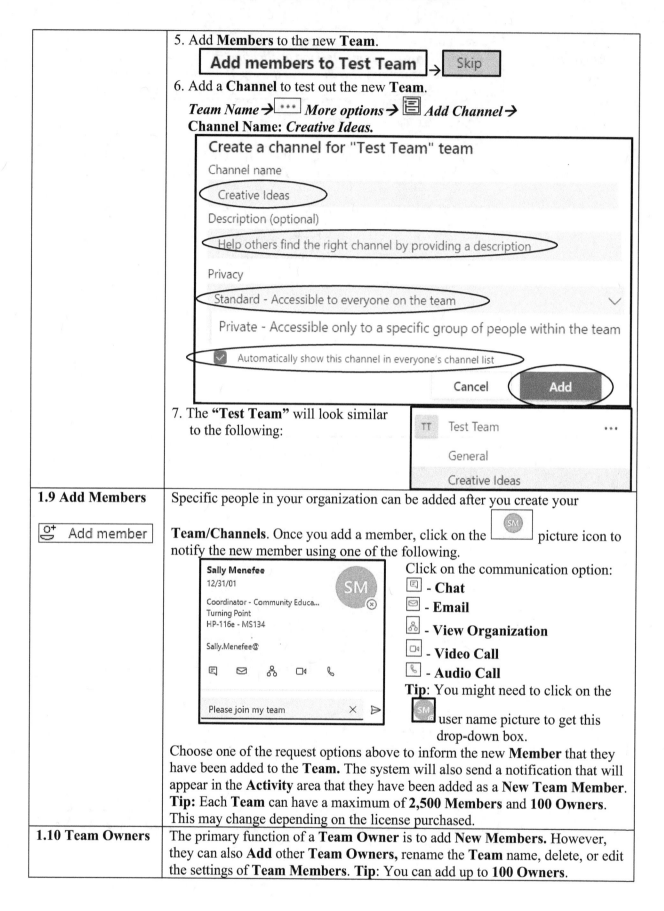 7. The **"Test Team"** will look similar to the following: TT Test Team ··· General Creative Ideas
1.9 Add Members 👤⁺ Add member	Specific people in your organization can be added after you create your **Team/Channels.** Once you add a member, click on the (SM) picture icon to notify the new member using one of the following. **Sally Menefee** 12/31/01 SM Coordinator - Community Educa... Turning Point HP-116e - MS134 Sally.Menefee@ 💬 ✉ 👥 📹 📞 Please join my team ✕ ➤ Click on the communication option: 💬 - **Chat** ✉ - **Email** 👥 - **View Organization** 📹 - **Video Call** 📞 - **Audio Call** **Tip**: You might need to click on the (SM) user name picture to get this drop-down box. Choose one of the request options above to inform the new **Member** that they have been added to the **Team.** The system will also send a notification that will appear in the **Activity** area that they have been added as a **New Team Member**. **Tip:** Each **Team** can have a maximum of **2,500 Members** and **100 Owners**. This may change depending on the license purchased.
1.10 Team Owners	The primary function of a **Team Owner** is to add **New Members**. However, they can also **Add** other **Team Owners**, rename the **Team** name, delete, or edit the settings of **Team Members**. **Tip**: You can add up to **100 Owners**.

1.11 Team Members	**Team Members** will be able to contribute content to the **Channels.** However, by default, you will not be able to **Add New Members** or **Owners.** **Tip**: You can add up to **2,500 Members.**
Practice Exercise 4 *Add Member*	You can add specific people to your organization after you create your **Team.** 1. *Click the* **Teams** *Button (located on the left side of the interface).* 2. **To add Team Member:** *Next to the "Test Team" name* → *Click the More Options* `...` → `Add member` 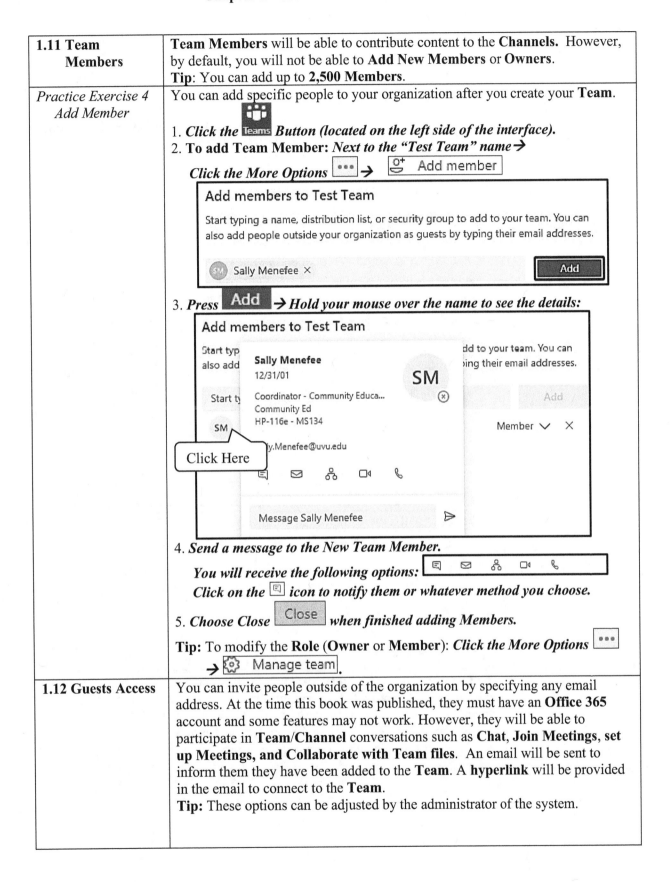 3. *Press* **Add** → *Hold your mouse over the name to see the details:* 4. *Send a message to the New Team Member.* *You will receive the following options:* 🗨 ✉ ⛾ ◻ ☎ *Click on the* 🗨 *icon to notify them or whatever method you choose.* 5. *Choose Close* `Close` *when finished adding Members.* **Tip:** To modify the **Role (Owner** or **Member**): *Click the More Options* `...` → ⚙ `Manage team`.
1.12 Guests Access	You can invite people outside of the organization by specifying any email address. At the time this book was published, they must have an **Office 365** account and some features may not work. However, they will be able to participate in **Team/Channel** conversations such as **Chat, Join Meetings, set up Meetings, and Collaborate with Team files.** An email will be sent to inform them they have been added to the **Team.** A **hyperlink** will be provided in the email to connect to the **Team.** **Tip:** These options can be adjusted by the administrator of the system.

	Display Name - When you create a new **Guest** by adding an email address, you can change the **Display Name** to be more friendly by selecting the 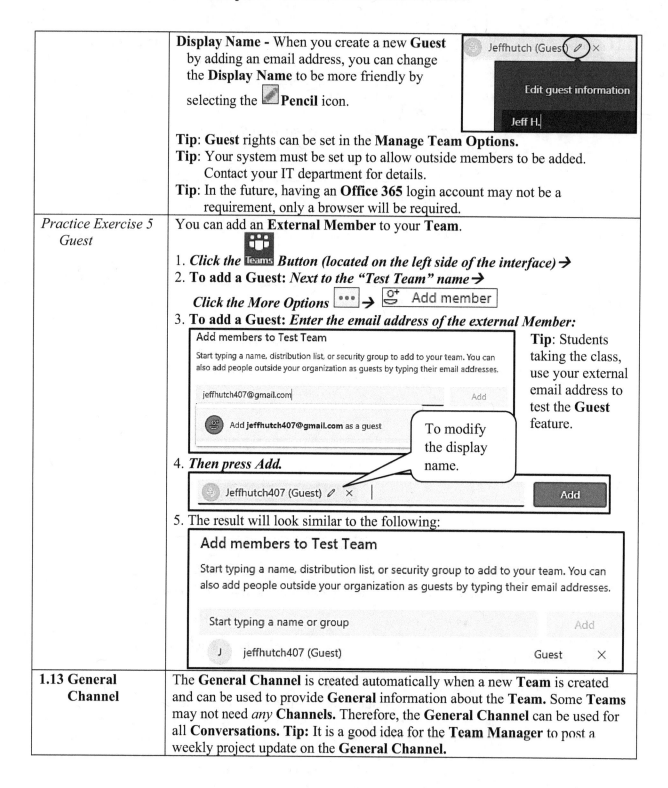 **Pencil** icon. **Tip**: **Guest** rights can be set in the **Manage Team Options.** **Tip**: Your system must be set up to allow outside members to be added. Contact your IT department for details. **Tip**: In the future, having an **Office 365** login account may not be a requirement, only a browser will be required.
Practice Exercise 5 *Guest*	You can add an **External Member** to your **Team.** 1. *Click the* [Teams] *Button (located on the left side of the interface)* → 2. **To add a Guest:** *Next to the "Test Team" name* → *Click the More Options* [...] → [Add member] 3. **To add a Guest:** *Enter the email address of the external Member:* **Tip**: Students taking the class, use your external email address to test the **Guest** feature. 4. *Then press Add.* To modify the display name. 5. The result will look similar to the following:
1.13 General Channel	The **General Channel** is created automatically when a new **Team** is created and can be used to provide **General** information about the **Team.** Some **Teams** may not need *any* **Channels.** Therefore, the **General Channel** can be used for all **Conversations. Tip:** It is a good idea for the **Team Manager** to post a weekly project update on the **General Channel.**

Practice Exercise 6
General Chat
	Enter a comment describing your understanding of the **Team** and **Channels**.
	
	1. *Click the* Teams *Button→ Select the Team name: Test Team→*
	   Select the Channel: *General.*
	2. *Enter a new message in the Compose New Message box→*
	   This Team is set up to test the Teams features. The Team is the Project and
	   the Channels are the tasks to be performed.
	
	This Team is set up to test the Teams features. The Team is the Project and the Channels are the tasks to be performed.
	A̶ 🖉 ☺ GIF 🖼 🎥 ⋯ ▷
	
	3. ***Press the Enter key to Send (Post) it.***

1.14 Show Teams
👁 Show
	This is a way to place the more important **Teams** on top and inactive **Teams** under the **More Options**. By default, all **Teams** are marked as 👁 **Show** and will always be visible on the top of the interface labeled as **Your Teams**. The following will be placed on top of the **Teams/Channels** area:
	
	▾ Your teams
	  TT Test Team ⋯
	
	▾ Favorites
	  TT Test Team
	
	Tip: This feature was previously called ⭐ **Favorites**.

1.15 Hide Teams 🚫 Hide	When you mark the **Team** as 🚫 **Hide,** it will **Move** a **Team** to the bottom of the list. When you use the ⋯ **More Options** you will be able to change it to 👁 Show. Hidden teams TT Team Template ⋯ More Options
Practice Exercise 7 *Show/Hide*	*Click the* Teams *Button (located on the left side of the interface)→Click on the Team name→ ⋯ More Options→* *Change the 🚫 Hide / 👁 Show Options status to observe the results.*

1.16 Add Channel	This will be covered in greater detail in Section 2 of this chapter. However, the option will allow **Members** to **Add New Channels** to the **Team.**	✐ Hide
1.17 Add Member	To **Add New Members:** *Select the Team name→... More Options→Add Member.*	⚙ Manage team
1.18 Leave The Team	If you no longer wish to be on the **Team**, choose this option. You can't leave if you are the last **Owner**. Therefore, you will need to assign another person as the **Owner**.	🗐 Add channel ⚲ Add member 🏃 Leave the team
1.19 Edit Team	This is used to change the **Team** name, description, and change the **Team** to **Public/Private.**	✎ Edit team
1.20 Get Link To Team	For a **Private Team**, this **Link** can be sent to a potential **Team Member** to connect to the **Team**. For a **Public Team**, this can be sent to anyone to join the **Public Team** automatically. Get a link to the team 29e-47cf-b70e-ab89b0589e24&tenantId=1ea2b65f-2f5e-440e-b025-dfdfafd8e097 Cancel Copy	🔗 Get link to team 🏷 Manage tags 🗑 Delete the team
Practice Exercise 8 Get Link To Team	1. *Click the* Teams *Button (located on the left side of the interface)→ Click on the Team name→* ⋯ *More Options→Get Link To Team→* Copy. Get a link to the team 29e-47cf-b70e-ab89b0589e24&tenantId=1ea2b65f-2f5e-440e-b025-dfdfafd8e097 Cancel Copy 2. *Open a Web Browser and paste the link.*	
1.21 Manage Tags	🏷 Manage tags **Tags** can be added to multiple members in order to easily connect with the right subset of people. **Team Owners** and **Members** (make sure the settings are enabled) can add one or more **Tags** to a person. The **Tags** can then be used in **@mentions** in a conversation by anyone on the **Team** in a **Channel** post with the **Tagged Member**. You can add up to 25 tags, and each tag can contain a maximum of 25 characters. The following is an example use: *A manager wants to post an announcement to a channel using a Tag so everyone assigned will be notified.*	
1.22 Tags Configuration	In the **Teams Admin Center**, you can control who can add tags and how tags are used. In the Microsoft Teams admin center (left side of navigation screen): *Org-wide settings→Teams settings.* **Tagging** Adding tags to your teams will make them more discoverable for people in your organization. Tagging is enabled for: Team owners ⌄ Team owner can override who can apply tags ○ Off Members can add additional tags ● On Suggested default tags ⓘ contoso × design × engineering ×	

1.23 Delete The Team 🗑	This is used to **Delete** the **Team** name and all the contents contained in the **Team**. You must be an **Owner** to perform this operation. Also, it will display a **Message** such as: Delete "Test Team" team Are you sure you want to delete the team "Test Team"? All channels, chats, files, and the Office 365 Group for this team will be deleted. ☐ I understand that everything will be deleted.
Student Project A Create a new team	In this student project, the students in the class will contribute the necessary (**Conversations** and documents) to set up a class located at a physical facility. The **Team/Channels** will be used to provide the necessary documentation needed to set up the class. The instructor (or one of the students) will create the **Team Name**. 1. *Click the* Teams *Button (located on the left side of the interface)→ Choose* Join or create a team → Create team → Other *Class →* 2. **Team Name: Microsoft Team Class** 3. **Description:** *This Team will be used to organize and deliver a physical Team's class.* 4. **Privacy:** *Private* → Next →*Add Members →(Enter student names in the class) →* Add → Close 5. *The final screen will look similar to the following:* Create your team Collaborate closely with a group of people inside your organization based on project, initiative, or common interest. Watch a quick overview Team name Microsoft Team Class ⊘ Description This Team will be used to organize and deliver a physical Teams class. Privacy Private - Only team owners can add members ⌄
1.24 Manage Team Members	This can be used to **Manage Teams Members:** *Click the* Teams *Button (located on the left side of the interface) Click on the Team Name →* ••• *More Options →* ⚙ *Manage Team →Members.* Members Pending Requests Channels Settings Apps *Members Tab.* This will allow you to change **Member** and **Owner** rights.

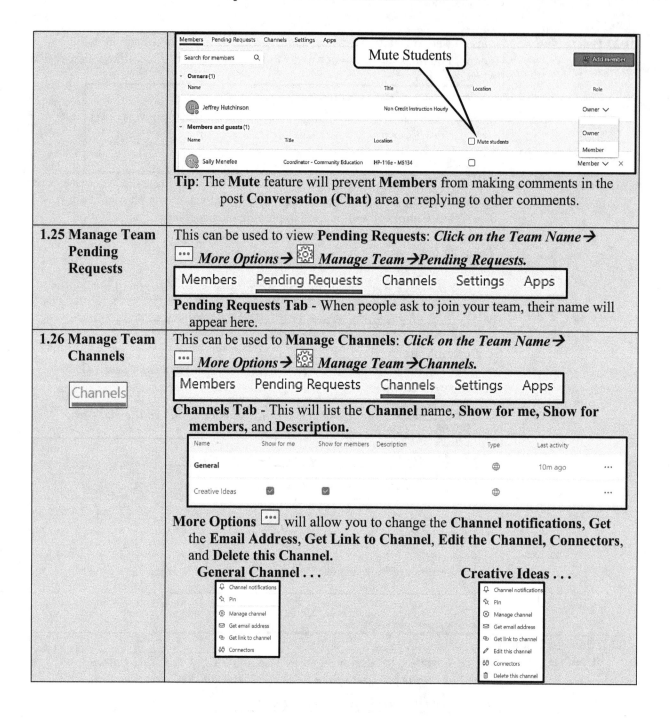

	Tip: The **Mute** feature will prevent **Members** from making comments in the post **Conversation (Chat)** area or replying to other comments.	
1.25 Manage Team Pending Requests	This can be used to view **Pending Requests**: *Click on the Team Name →* ⋯ *More Options →* ⚙ *Manage Team →Pending Requests.* Members Pending Requests Channels Settings Apps **Pending Requests Tab** - When people ask to join your team, their name will appear here.	
1.26 Manage Team Channels Channels	This can be used to **Manage Channels**: *Click on the Team Name →* ⋯ *More Options →* ⚙ *Manage Team →Channels.* Members Pending Requests Channels Settings Apps **Channels Tab** - This will list the **Channel** name, **Show for me, Show for members,** and **Description.** **More Options** ⋯ will allow you to change the **Channel notifications, Get the Email Address, Get Link to Channel, Edit the Channel, Connectors,** and **Delete this Channel.**	

1.27 Manage Team Settings
 	
Settings
	This can be used to **Manage Team Settings**: *Click on the Team Name →* ⋯ *More Options →* ⚙ *Manage Team → Settings.*
	
	Members Pending Requests Channels Settings Apps
	
	Settings - This will change the behavior of **Teams**.
	   Add Team Picture - Add a **Picture** for your **Team**.
	      Choose Change Picture.
	
	▾ **Team picture** Add a team picture
	
	TT
	
	⬆ Change picture
	
	Member Permissions - This will change what **Members** can do. Enable **Channel** creation, adding **Apps**, and more:
	
	▾ Member permissions Enable channel creation, adding apps, and more
	Allow members to create and update channels ☑
	Allow members to create private channels ☑
	Allow members to delete and restore channels ☑
	Allow members to add and remove apps ☑
	Allow members to upload custom apps ☑
	Allow members to create, update, and remove tabs ☑
	Allow members to create, update, and remove connectors ☑
	Owners can delete all messages ☑
	Give members the option to delete their messages ☑
	Give members the option to edit their messages ☑
	
	☐ Allow creating and updating **Channels**.
	☐ Allow **Members** to delete and restore **Channels**.
	☐ Allow **Members** to add and remove **Apps**.
	☐ Allow **Members** to create, update, and remove tabs.
	☐ Allow **Members** to create, update, and remove connectors.
	☑ **Owners** can delete all messages.
	☑ Give **Members** the option to delete their messages.
	☑ Give **Members** the option to edit their messages.
	Tip: All the options above can be checked for class purposes, but needs to be carefully thought out for implementation.
	General Channel: (Choose only one option):
	   ⬤ Anyone can post messages.
	   ○ Anyone can post; show an alert that posting will notify everyone (recommended for large teams).
	   ○ Only owners can post messages.
	Guest Permissions - This will only appear when a **Guest** is added to your **Team**. A **Guest** (external user) is someone who is outside the organization and added to the **Team** by providing their **Email** address.
	Enable Channel Creation:
	
	▾ Guest permissions Enable channel creation
	Allow guests to to create and update channels ☐
	Allow guests to delete channels ☐

☐ Allow Creating and **Updating Channels**.

☐ Allow **Guests** to **Delete Channels**.

@mentions - Choose who can use @team and @channel mentions.

▾ @mentions	Choose who can use @team and @channel mentions	
	Show members the option to @team or @[team name] (this will send a notification to everyone on the team)	☑
	Give members the option to @channel or @[channel name]. This will notify everyone who's shown the mentioned channel in their channel lists.	☑

☑ Show **Members** the option to @team or @[team name] (this will send a notification to everyone on the team).

☑ Show **Members** the option to @channel or @[channel name] (this will send a notification to everyone who has **Favorited** the **Channel** being mentioned).

Team Code - Share this **Code** so people can join the **Team** directly - you won't get join requests.

▾ Team code	Share this code so people can join the team directly - you won't get join requests
	Generate
	Note: Guests won't be able to join with a team code

Tip: Guests won't be able to join with a

Team Code. Generate → 🗋 Copy → *Teams* → *Choose*

👥⁺ Join or create a team *Located on the lower left side* →

Then paste the code in the Enter code *box.*

Fun Stuff - Allow emoji, memes, GIFs, or stickers.

▾ Fun stuff	Allow emoji, memes, GIFs, or stickers	
	Giphy	
	Enable Giphy for this team	☑
	Filter out inappropriate content using one of the setting below:	
	Moderate ⌄ ⓘ	
	Stickers and memes	
	Enable stickers and memes	☑
	Custom Memes	
	Allow memes to be uploaded	☑

Giphy: ☑ Enable **Giphy** for this **Team**.

Filter out inappropriate content using one of the **Settings** below:

Stickers and memes:

☑ Enable **Stickers** and **Memes**.

Custom Memes:

☐ Allow **Memes** to be uploaded.

Who can add Tags:

▾ Tags	Choose who can add tags
	Who can add tags
	All members ⌄
	Owners only

1.28 Analytics Analytics	This provides statistics concerning your overall team usage: 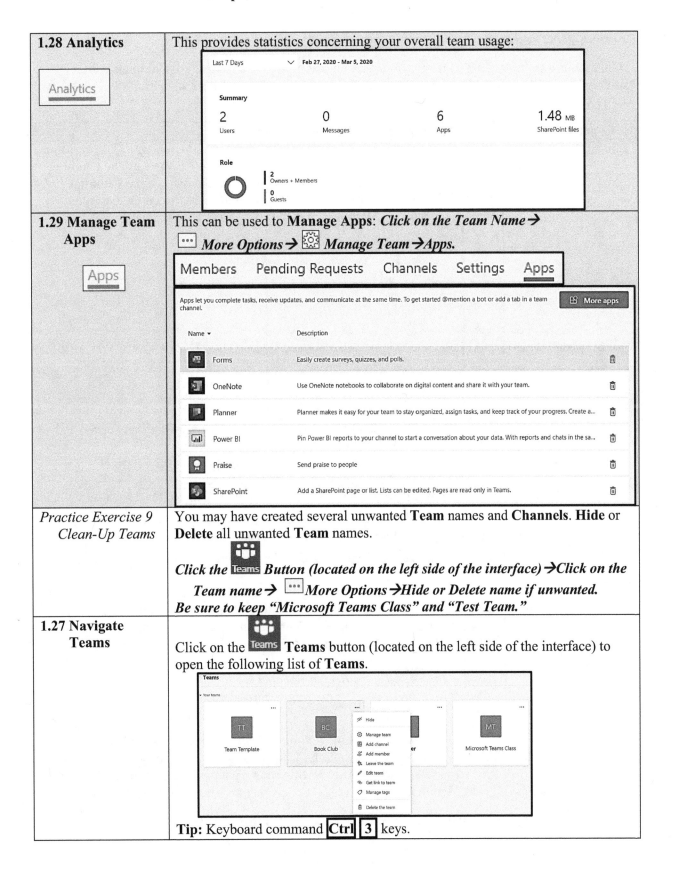
1.29 Manage Team Apps Apps	This can be used to **Manage Apps:** *Click on the Team Name →* ⋯ *More Options →* ⚙ *Manage Team → Apps.*
Practice Exercise 9 Clean-Up Teams	You may have created several unwanted **Team** names and **Channels**. **Hide** or **Delete** all unwanted **Team** names. *Click the* 📋 *Button (located on the left side of the interface) → Click on the Team name →* ⋯ *More Options → Hide or Delete name if unwanted.* **Be sure to keep "Microsoft Teams Class" and "Test Team."**
1.27 Navigate Teams	Click on the 📋 **Teams** button (located on the left side of the interface) to open the following list of **Teams**. **Tip:** Keyboard command **Ctrl** **3** keys.

Section 2 - Channels

A **Channel** is a subtask of a **Team** name or an action that needs to be completed. **Channels** contain **Conversations**, files, etc. If you join the **Team** late, then you can review the **Conversation** to get up to speed on the **Channel**.

Concept	Explanation / *Command String in italic.*
1.30 Add Channel	The next step is to add a **Channel**. Each **Channel** has a separate **Conversation (Chat)** room to converse with **Team Members** in the **Channel**. The **Channel** name should be a focused topic discussing a specific issue. If the **Channel** name is too broad, contributions may be difficult to follow. If the **Channel** name is too narrow, **Members** may have few ideas to contribute. In some cases, the default **General Channel** is the only **Channel** needed and will contain the **Team Conversation**. **Tip**: It is a good idea to add a **Message Post** in the **General Channel** to describe what the **Team** has been set up to accomplish.
1.31 Team Member Channels	All **Team Members** can create new **Channels** as long as it has been set up in the **Manage Team Options.** **Tip**: **To add this feature:** *Click on the Team Name → ⋯ More Options → ⚙ Manage Team → Settings → ☑* Allow **Members** to delete and restore **Channels.**
Practice Exercise 10 Create a Channel	In the previous practice exercise, you created a **Test Team**. Have each student add random channel names such as **Testing Channel, How does this work?, Test 1, Test 2**, etc. If multiple students are in the class have them put their initials at the end of the **Channel** name. 1. *Select the Teams Button (located on the left side of the interface) → Select the "Test Team" (or create it if necessary).* 2. *⋯ More Options.* 3. *Add Channel → Channel Name: Creative Ideas(initials) →* Create. **Tip:** If multiple people are adding **Channels,** be sure to append your initials.
1.32 Channel Notifications 🔔	When you select the **Channel Notifications**, you will get notifications when a **Team Member** adds a message to the **Conversation (Chat)** area. This notification will be located in the Activity **Button** (located on the left side of the interface). To disable the **Channel Notifications**: *Click on Channel name → ⋯ More Options → 🔔* Channel notifications

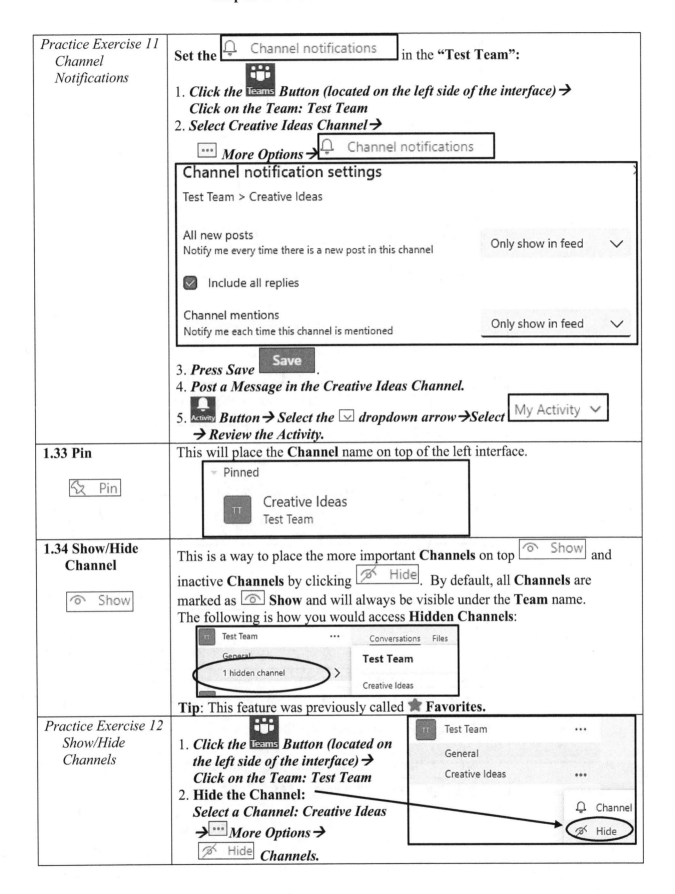

Practice Exercise 11 *Channel* *Notifications*	**Set the** ⌗ Channel notifications **in the "Test Team":** 1. **Click the** Teams **Button (located on the left side of the interface)→ Click on the Team: Test Team** 2. **Select Creative Ideas Channel→** ⋯ **More Options →** ⌗ Channel notifications **Channel notification settings** Test Team > Creative Ideas All new posts Notify me every time there is a new post in this channel — Only show in feed ∨ ☑ Include all replies Channel mentions Notify me each time this channel is mentioned — Only show in feed ∨ 3. **Press Save** Save . 4. **Post a Message in the Creative Ideas Channel.** 5. Activity **Button→ Select the** ∨ **dropdown arrow→Select** My Activity ∨ **→ Review the Activity.**
1.33 Pin ⚲ Pin	This will place the **Channel** name on top of the left interface. ⌄ Pinned TT Creative Ideas Test Team
1.34 Show/Hide Channel 👁 Show	This is a way to place the more important **Channels** on top 👁 Show and inactive **Channels** by clicking ⌀ Hide . By default, all **Channels** are marked as 👁 **Show** and will always be visible under the **Team** name. The following is how you would access **Hidden Channels**: TT Test Team ⋯ Conversations Files General **Test Team** 1 hidden channel > Creative Ideas **Tip**: This feature was previously called ★ **Favorites.**
Practice Exercise 12 *Show/Hide* *Channels*	1. **Click the** Teams **Button (located on the left side of the interface)→ Click on the Team: Test Team** 2. **Hide the Channel:** **Select a Channel: Creative Ideas →** ⋯ **More Options →** ⌀ Hide **Channels.** TT Test Team ⋯ General Creative Ideas ⋯ ⌗ Channel ⌀ Hide

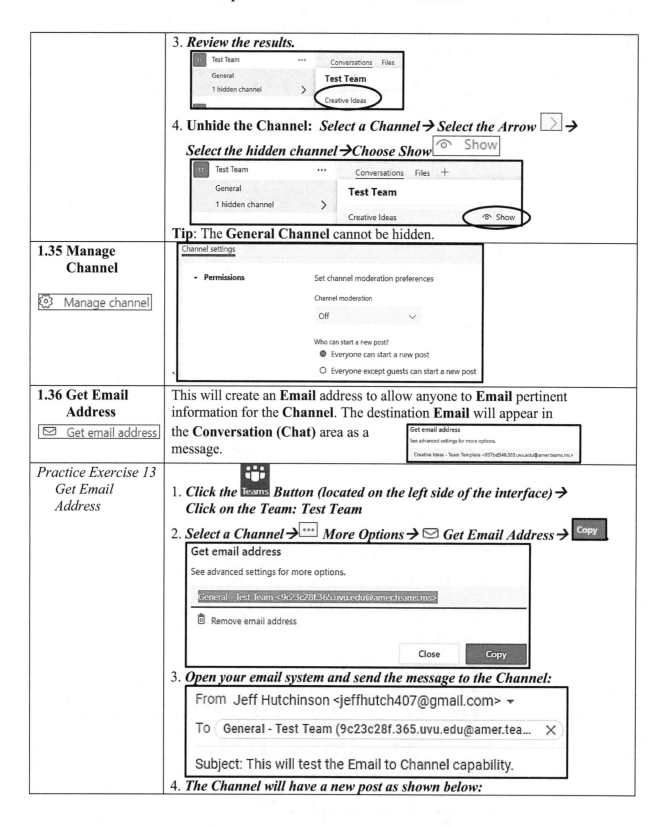

	3. *Review the results.*
	4. Unhide the Channel: *Select a Channel→ Select the Arrow →* *Select the hidden channel→Choose Show*
	Tip: The **General Channel** cannot be hidden.
1.35 Manage Channel Manage channel	Channel settings ▾ **Permissions** Set channel moderation preferences Channel moderation Off Who can start a new post? ⦿ Everyone can start a new post ◯ Everyone except guests can start a new post
1.36 Get Email Address ✉ Get email address	This will create an **Email** address to allow anyone to **Email** pertinent information for the **Channel**. The destination **Email** will appear in the **Conversation (Chat)** area as a message. Get email address See advanced settings for more options. Creative Ideas - Team Template <857bd348.365.uvu.edu@amer.teams.ms>
Practice Exercise 13 Get Email Address	1. *Click the* Teams *Button (located on the left side of the interface) →* *Click on the Team: Test Team* 2. *Select a Channel→ More Options → ✉ Get Email Address →* Copy Get email address See advanced settings for more options. General - Test Team <9c23c28f.365.uvu.edu@amer.teams.ms> 🗑 Remove email address Close Copy 3. *Open your email system and send the message to the Channel:* From Jeff Hutchinson <jeffhutch407@gmail.com> ▾ To (General - Test Team (9c23c28f.365.uvu.edu@amer.tea... ✕ Subject: This will test the Email to Channel capability. 4. *The Channel will have a new post as shown below:*

	jeffhutch407@gmail.com 7:39 PM To General - Test Team Subject: This will test the Email to Channel capability. -- Jeff Hutchinson (801) 376-6687
	5. Review the **Channel** to see if an email was posted. **Tip**: There may be a delay to display the message.
1.37 Get Link To Channel ⟲ Get link to channel	This will generate a **Link** that will open the **Channel**. The **Link** can be emailed to someone to go directly to the **Channel**. **Tip**: You will need to login in order to see the **Microsoft Teams**. Get a link to the channel 01ac-4aee-892f-555e5919b6e58&tenantId=1ea2b65f-2f5e-440e-b025-dfdfafd8e097 Cancel Copy
Practice Exercise 14 *Get Link To Channel*	1. *Click the* Teams *Button (located on the left side of the interface)* → *Click on the Team: Test Team* 2. *Select a Channel* → *More Options* → *Get Link To Channel.* 3. Copy *Copy the Link.* 4. *Close and log out of the Teams application.* 5. *Paste the link in a web browser.*
1.38 Edit This Channel ✎ Edit this channel	This will allow you to **Edit** the **Channel Name** and **Description**.
Practice Exercise 15 *Edit Channel*	1. *Click the* Teams *Button (located on the left side of the interface)* → *Click on the Team: Test Team.* 2. **Select a Channel:** *Creative Ideas* → *More Options* → *Edit This Channel.* 3. *Change the Description of the Channel.* Edit "Creative Ideas" channel in "Microsoft Teams Class" team Channel name Creative Ideas Description (optional) Help others find the right channel by providing a description ☑ Automatically show this channel in everyone's channel list
1.39 Connectors 🔌 Connectors	This is a great way to push your external **App** content into **Microsoft Teams**. Any user can **Connect** to services like **Trello**, **GitHub**, **Bing News**, or **Twitter** and get notified of the **Team's Activity** in that service. 🔌 Connectors **Tip**: **To allow this feature:** *Click on the Team Name* → *More Options* → ⚙ *Manage Team* → *Settings* → ☑ **Allow Members** to create, update, and remove connectors.

Practice Exercise 16 Connector	The following will create an **NPR News Feed** which will update in the **Creative Ideas** post every 6 hours. 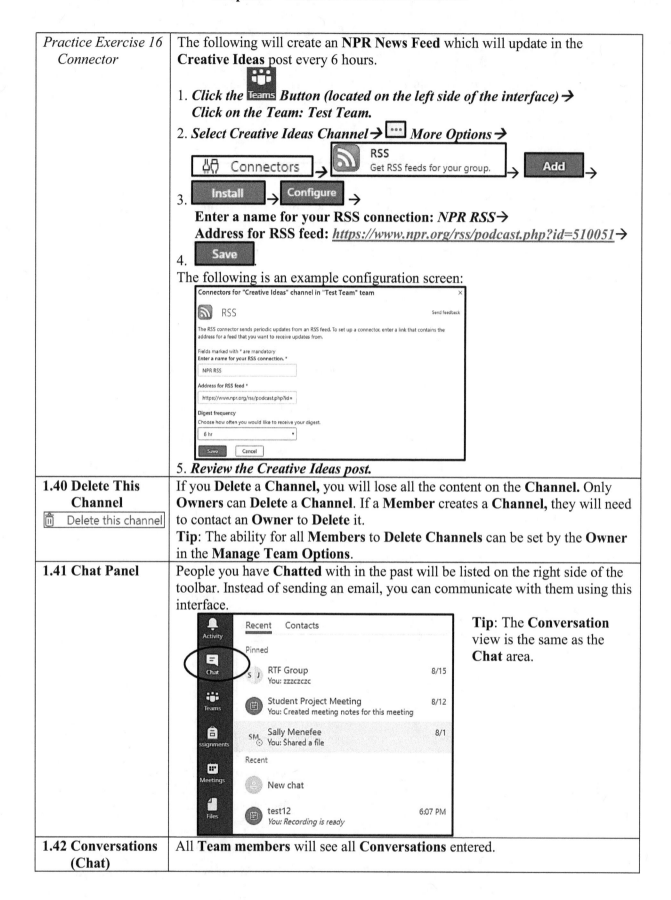
1.40 Delete This Channel 🗑 Delete this channel	If you **Delete** a **Channel,** you will lose all the content on the **Channel.** Only **Owners** can **Delete** a **Channel.** If a **Member** creates a **Channel,** they will need to contact an **Owner** to **Delete** it. **Tip**: The ability for all **Members** to **Delete Channels** can be set by the **Owner** in the **Manage Team Options**.
1.41 Chat Panel	People you have **Chatted** with in the past will be listed on the right side of the toolbar. Instead of sending an email, you can communicate with them using this interface.
1.42 Conversations (Chat)	All **Team members** will see all **Conversations** entered.

1.43 Video Meetings	This will allow a **Team Member** assigned to a **Team/Channel** to start a **Video Meeting** at any time. Anyone who is a **Member,** but not in the current conversation, can jump into the **Meeting** when they see it actively running. This can be done while you are in the **Conversation (Chat)** area. **In the Conversation screen:** *Choose* *Meet Now→* **Tip**: you can also **Schedule Meetings** from within the **Chat Button.** The person who set up the **Video Call** will be in the lower right small box: Meeting Organizer **Tip**: This feature will be covered in a later chapter.

Student Project B *Create Channels*	This student project will create the **Channels** used for the **Microsoft Teams Class** (created in previous student projects). Each student will pick a **Channel** from the list below and add their initials at the end of the name. We will be using your designated **Channel** name at a later time to make changes. Each student will contribute to all **Channels** at any time.
	
	Select the *Teams Button (located on the left side of the interface)→* *Select the "Microsoft Teams Class" (or create it if necessary)→* *More Options→* *Add Channel→ New Channel (initials)→* **Create**.
	
	Enter the **Channel Names:**
	  Schedule Location(initials)
	  Lunch Coordination(initials)
	  Computer Coordination(initials)
	  Courseware(initials)
	  Date Availability(initials)
	Optional Channels - If there are more than 5 students in the class, then add the following **Channels:**
	  Topics to cover(initials)
	  Students to Notify(initials)
	  Other Possible Classes
	Add additional **Channels** as desired.

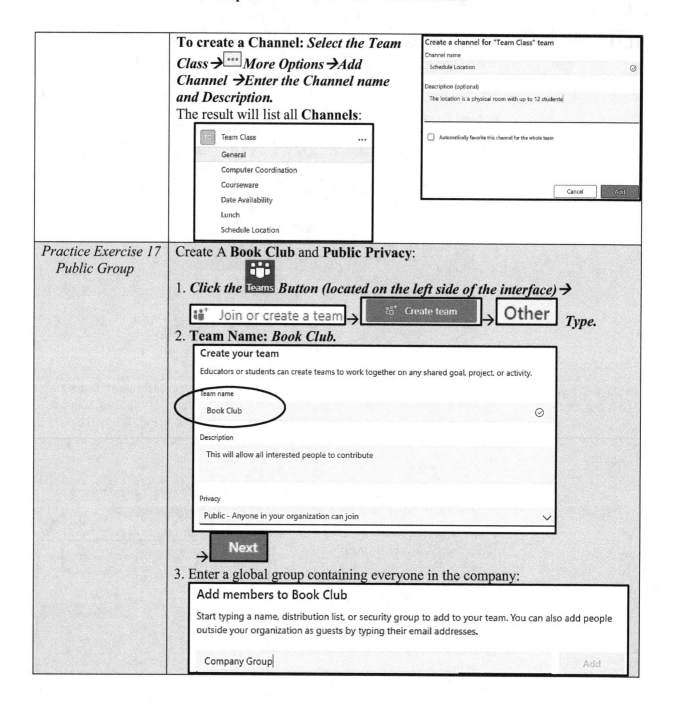

	To create a Channel: *Select the Team Class →* ··· *More Options →Add Channel →Enter the Channel name and Description.* The result will list all **Channels**:
Practice Exercise 17 Public Group	Create A **Book Club** and **Public Privacy**: 1. ***Click the* Teams *Button (located on the left side of the interface) →*** Join or create a team → Create team → Other *Type.* 2. **Team Name:** *Book Club.* 3. Enter a global group containing everyone in the company:

Create a channel for "Team Class" team

Channel name

Schedule Location

Description (optional)

The location is a physical room with up to 12 students

☐ Automatically favorite this channel for the whole team

Cancel   Add

Team Class   ...
General
Computer Coordination
Courseware
Date Availability
Lunch
Schedule Location

Create your team

Educators or students can create teams to work together on any shared goal, project, or activity.

Team name

Book Club

Description

This will allow all interested people to contribute

Privacy

Public - Anyone in your organization can join

Next

Add members to Book Club

Start typing a name, distribution list, or security group to add to your team. You can also add people outside your organization as guests by typing their email addresses.

Company Group   Add

Chapter 2 - Conversations (Chat)

This will allow **Team Members** to provide communication in a specific **Channel** and allow other **Team Members** to respond. All the standard features of **Chatting** are supported including **Reply** to a comment, use of **Emojis**, as well as **Stamps** and **Animated Gifs**. Also, you can have a **Conversation (Chat)** at a

Global level with anyone in the organization using the [Chat] **Chat Button** or press Ctrl 2 keys.

Chapter Contents:

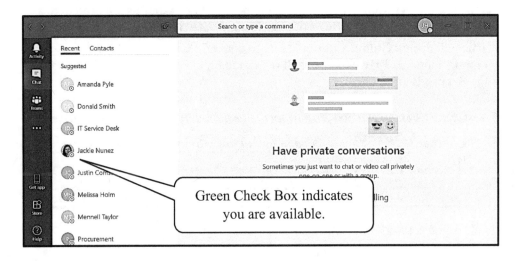

Section 1 - Global Private Chat

The **Global Chat Button** is located on the left side of the interface and is used as a **Private Chat** with one or more people within the organization. This **Conversation** will be completely independent of the **Team.** Furthermore, **Private Conversation** is not searchable by others because it is **Private.**

Concept	Explanation / *Command String in italic.*
2.1 Chat Button	**Chat** *Button →Conversation Tab →Select a Contact →* *(Review the icons in the upper right corner) →* **Start Video Meeting** **Make a Phone Call** **Start Sharing Your Screen** **Add People** **Tip**: A **Conversation** is usually multiple people, but a **Chat** usually refers to a private **Conversation.** **Tip**: Keyboard command `Ctrl` `2` keys.
2.2 New Chat	This will open a **Global Chat** interface to converse with anyone in the organization in a **Private** session. It is located on the top of the interface next to the **Search Box**. **To Chat:** *Click on the* **Chat** *Button located on the left side of the interface →* *Choose* **Contacts** ⌄ *dropdown arrow →Select the desired name →.* Single Click — SM Sally Menefee *The following Chat box will appear on the lower portion of the interface:* Type your questions here **Pop Out Chat** - When you double click on the name above it will open the **Pop Out Chat interface.** **Configuration Alternative** - Some systems provide the following icons above the **Chatbox.** ▢ **Chat** - Start a **Conversation (Chat).** ✉ **Email** - Send an **Email.** ⬚ **View Organization** - Optional may not be supported. ▢ **Video Call** - Start a **Video Call.** ☎ **Audio Call** - Start an **Audio Call.** Sally 12/31/01 SM — Coordinator - Community Educa... Turning Point HP-116e - MS134 — Message Sally l Message Sally l — select or highlight a name in the **Contacts Area.** ▷ **Send** - Type your **Message** in the box provided and press the ▷**Send** icon or press the **Enter** key on the keyboard to post the message. **Tip**: When a new person is added to an existing private **Chat** session, the **Private Conversation** comments are not available to a newly added person.
2.3 Add People	When you **Add** a **New Person** to an existing **Private Conversation,** it will start a new thread and the previous **Conversation** will remain **Private.** **To add a new person:** *Click on the* **Add People Button** *(located in the upper right corner of the interface).*

2.4 Contacts	The **Contacts Tab** is located on the upper left side of the interface. Recent Contacts Activity Favorites ... Chat SM Sally Menefee Additional **Contacts** can be added by pressing: Create a new contact group (located in the lower-left corner of the interface).
2.5 Message Area	This is the **Message Area** where you can begin a **New Chat**. Type a new message Schedule A Meeting - This icon is different compared to the icon used in the **Channel Conversation** area.
Practice Exercise 18 *Private Chat*	This will start a **Chat** with a specific person in a **Private** setting, meaning that nobody else will be able to join the **Chat** session. 1. **To Start A Private Chat:** *Select Chat Button (located on the left side of the interface)→Select the name (in Recent or Contacts Tab).* 2. *Enter a new message in the Compose New Message box→ Press the Enter key to Send it or press the ▷ Send (Post) icon.* Type a new message **Tip**: Locate someone in the class and start a **Private Conversation**.
Practice Exercise 19 *Group Chat*	This will allow you to have a **Conversation** with multiple people. 1. **To Start A Group Chat:** *Select Chat Button (located on the left side of the interface)→Select Add People icon located in the top right→ Add multiple people.* 2. *Enter a new message in the Compose New Message box→ Press the Enter key to Send it or press the ▷ Send (Post) icon.* Type a new message
2.6 Group	A **Group** can be created in order to make it easier to begin a new **Conversation (Chat)** with the same **Group** of people.

Practice Exercise 20 Create A Group	To create a **Group Conversation (Chat):** 1. **To Start A Group Conversation:** *Select* **Chat** *Button (located on the left side of the interface)* → 2. *Start a New Chat by pressing the* ✍ *icon or Contacts Tab* → ᐧᐧ⁺ Create a new contact group 3. *Enter the names to attend the Conversation (Chat) session:* To: SM Sally Menefee ✕ J jeffhutch407 (Guest) ✕ 🎥 📞 ⬆ ⌄ 4. **Press the** ⌄ **dropdown arrow on the right side→ Enter the Group name.** Group name: Test Group _____ To: SM Sally Menefee ✕ J jeffhutch407 (Guest) ✕ 5. *Press the Enter Key and Start Chatting.*
2.7 Previous Conversation	This is located on the left side of the interface next to the **Chat** **Chat Button.** If you no longer want to be part of a **Conversation (Chat):** **Mark As Unread** - The selected item will turn bold. **Pin/Unpin** - This will move the **Conversation** to the top of the list under the category **Pinned.** Otherwise, it will be listed under **Recent.** **Mute** - No longer receive notifications. **Hide** - Don't display it on top. **Manage Apps** - This will allow you to change the properties of an App. **Leave** - Remove yourself from the **Conversation.** 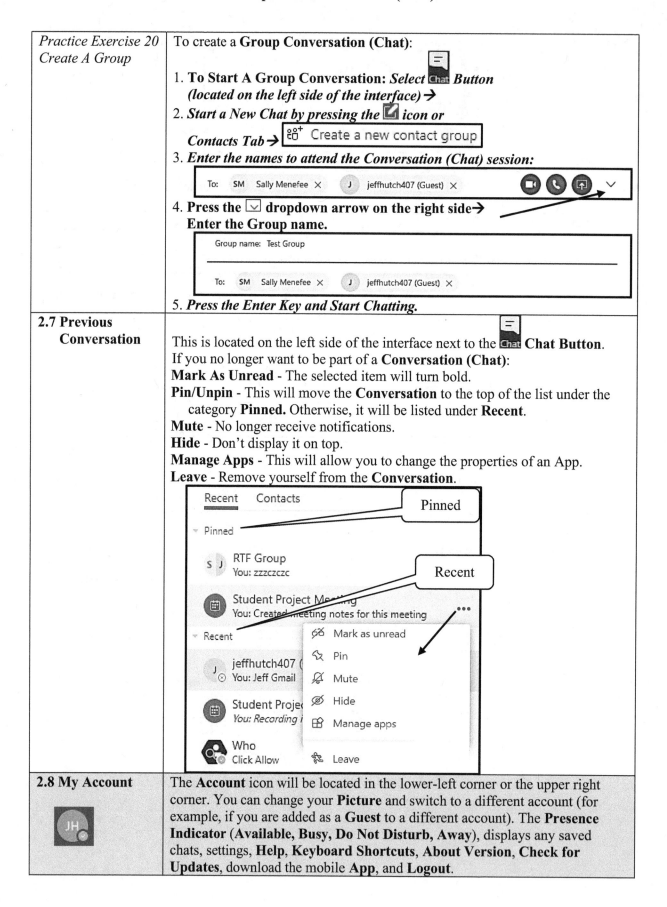
2.8 My Account JH	The **Account** icon will be located in the lower-left corner or the upper right corner. You can change your **Picture** and switch to a different account (for example, if you are added as a **Guest** to a different account). The **Presence Indicator (Available, Busy, Do Not Disturb, Away)**, displays any saved chats, settings, **Help, Keyboard Shortcuts, About Version, Check for Updates**, download the mobile **App**, and **Logout.**

Section 2 - Channel Conversation

This section will focus on the **Channel Conversation (Chat)** feature which will allow anyone on the **Team** to contribute to a **Conversation (Chat).** The **Chat Message** is sometimes called a **Post** or **Conversation** and anyone can **Reply** to your **Chat Message.** Also, we will cover format and status controls inside the **Message Area.**

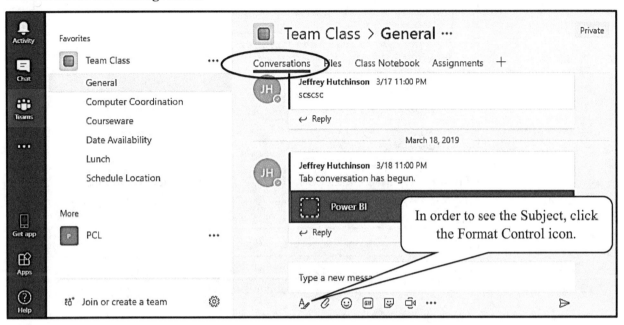

Concept	Explanation / *Command String in italic.*
2.9 Channel Chat	This will open a **Channel Chat** with anyone on the **Team**. All **Team Members** can participate at any time. **To Chat:** *Click on the* Teams *Button →Click on the Team name →Channels Name →Type your message in the Message area (located on the right) → Press the Enter key to Send it or press the* ▷ *Send (Post) icon.* Start a new conversation. Type @ to mention someone. A! 𝒞 ☺ GIF 🙂 📑 ▷ 💡 ··· ▷ **Tip**: All **Team Members** can participate in all **Channels**.
2.10 Message Area	This is the **Message Area** where you start a **Conversation (Chat).** This is the Message area A! 𝒞 ☺ GIF 🙂 📑 ▷ 💡 ··· ▷

Practice Exercise 21
General Chat
	Open the **"Test Team"** and the **General Channel** to **Post a Message**.
	
	1. *Click the* [Teams] *Button→ Select the Team name: Test Team→*
	   Select the Channel: *General.*
	2. *Start adding to the Conversation (Chat) by clicking on the message box:*
	
	   Type a new message
	   A ! ⊘ ☺ GIF 🙂 📷 ▷ ♀ ... ▷
	
	3. *Press the Enter key to Send it or press the ▷ Send (Post) icon.*
	   Possible messages to type in the Message box are:
	     Testing the Chat feature
	     My first Chat Conversation.
	     I understand how to use the Channel Chat.

2.11 Meet Now	This will allow you to have a face to face **Video Call** with someone or complete an **Audio Call**.
	
	To Start A Video Chat: *Click the* [Teams] *Button→Select a Team name→Select a Channel name→Select the Message Chat →Select* 📹 *Video Call under the message box.*
	
	   Start a new conversation. Type @ to mention someone.
	   A ! ⊘ ☺ GIF 🙂 📷 ▷ ♀ ... ▷

2.12 Add A Subject	When you create your message, add a **Subject** to better identify the content.
	
	Click on the [A] *Format Control to enter a Subject.*
	
	Type the **Subject** on the first line. **Format** AA it a large font and B **Bold.**
	
	   Add a subject
	
	   Start a new conversation. Type @ to mention someone.

2.13 Message Enhancement	This is located under the **Message** area and provides the following capabilities:
	![toolbar]
	Format Controls - This will allow you to type a **Subject**.
	! **Set Delivery Options -** This puts an icon on the side of a message.
	🗨 Standard - This is the default icon.
	! Important - This puts a **Red Strike** on the side of a message and displays the word **Important** on top of the post.
	🔔 Urgent - The recipients will be notified every 2 min for 20 min.
	Attach - This is the **Paper Clip** icon that **Attaches** a **File** from a local drive, **OneDrive**, or browses in **Teams/Channels**.
	Tip: This can also be used to point to an important prior post.
	Emoji - Your **Team** can provide **Animated Emotional** responses to your **Chat** session by using **Emojis**.
	Giphy - These are animated images to communicate a clear **Emotional** message.
	Sticker - These are small pictures that can be added to the **Conversation (Chat)** to communicate a clearer message.
	Meme - This new concept allows you to pick a picture and type a text message on the picture.
	Schedule a meeting - These will open the **Meeting Schedule** screen.
	Praise - This will identify a person you want to **Praise**.
	Message Extensions - This will allow you to add additional **Apps**.
	Send - This will **Send (Post)** a message or press the **Enter** key to **Send** it.
Practice Exercise 22 Graphic Image	1. *Click the* **Teams** *Button → Select the Team name:* *Test Team* → **Select the Channel:** *General.*
	2. *Start adding to the Conversation (Chat) by clicking on the message box:*
	Type a new message
	3. *Format Control → Add the following message Subject:* **Subject:** *Testing Emoji Graphics.*
	4. **Emoji:** *(Add an Emoji of your choice).*
	5. *Create several messages by repeat this process for* **Giphy,** *Sticker, and Meme*
	6. *Press the Enter key to Send it or press the Send (Post) icon.*

2.14 Format Controls 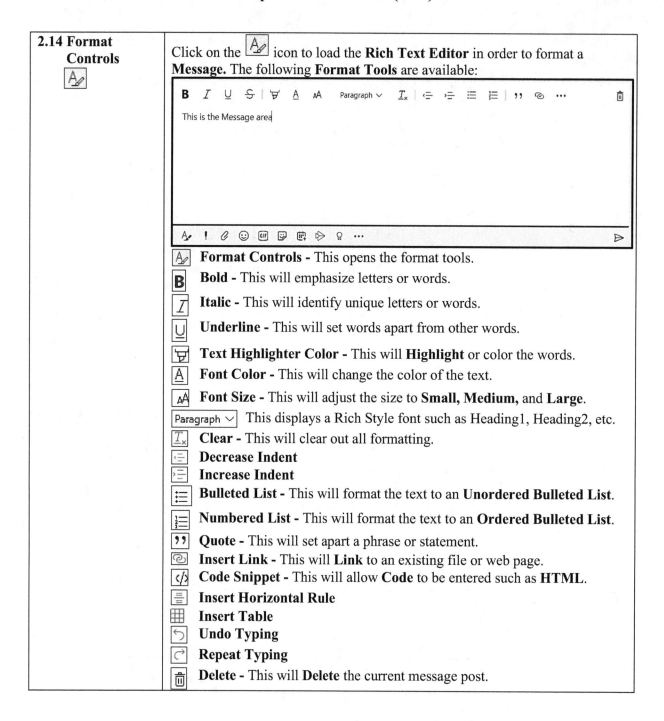	Click on the icon to load the **Rich Text Editor** in order to format a **Message.** The following **Format Tools** are available:

Format Controls - This opens the format tools.

Bold - This will emphasize letters or words.

Italic - This will identify unique letters or words.

Underline - This will set words apart from other words.

Text Highlighter Color - This will **Highlight** or color the words.

Font Color - This will change the color of the text.

Font Size - This will adjust the size to **Small, Medium,** and **Large.**

Paragraph ⌄ This displays a Rich Style font such as Heading1, Heading2, etc.

Clear - This will clear out all formatting.

Decrease Indent

Increase Indent

Bulleted List - This will format the text to an **Unordered Bulleted List.**

Numbered List - This will format the text to an **Ordered Bulleted List.**

Quote - This will set apart a phrase or statement.

Insert Link - This will **Link** to an existing file or web page.

Code Snippet - This will allow **Code** to be entered such as **HTML.**

Insert Horizontal Rule

Insert Table

Undo Typing

Repeat Typing

Delete - This will **Delete** the current message post.

Practice Exercise 23
Format Controls
	1. *Click the* [Teams] *Button→Select the Team name: Test Team→*
	   Select the Channel: *General.*
	2. *Start adding to the Conversation (Chat) by clicking on the message box:*
	   Enter the Message: *The Format Controls I will be testing are:*
	
	   Type a new message
	   A̲ꞎ ! 𝒸 ☺ [GIF] 🗋 🗓 ⋯ ▷
	
	3. [A̲] *Format Control →Add the following message Subject:*
	   Subject: *Format Controls* *(Format the subject to be Bold).*
	4. **Use some of the Format Controls above.**
	5. *Press the Enter key to Send it or press the ▷ Send (Post) icon.*
	Tip: Have each student choose different **Format Controls** so you can see the
	   results in the **Message Post.**

2.15 @mention	This is used to send an alert to a special person. It can also be used to bring attention to someone who may have an interest in the conversation or to alert people who may not be using the system and spark their interest. **To Alert someone:** *Include @MemberName with your message→The* *Member will receive an Alert.* **Tip**: **@mention** options can be disabled in the **Manage Team Options.**

Practice Exercise 24
@mention
	1. *Click the* [Teams] *Button→Select the Team name: Test Team→*
	   Select the Channel: *General.*
	2. *Click the format control icon→Enter the following message:*
	   Subject: *Mention*
	   Message: *The best graphics image entered was done by @UserName.*
	   (Type the name of the user above).
	
	   This is another test ☺ Suggestions
	   ↵ Reply (SM) Sally Menefee
	
	   The best graphic image entered was done by @
	   A̲ 𝒸 ☺ [GIF] 🗋 🖵 ⋯
	
	3. *Press the Enter key to Send it or press the ▷ Send (Post) icon.*
	4. Have the user check the [Activity] **Button.**

2.16 Leave Chat	This will exit or end the **Conversation (Chat).**
2.17 Video Call 📹	This will allow you to have a face to face **Video Call** with someone. **To Start A Video Chat:** *Select the Contact→* *Select* 📹 *Video Call on the top right.*
2.18 Audio Call 📞	This will allow you to have a **Phone Call** with someone. **To Start A Audio Chat:** *Select the Contact→* *Select* 📞 *Audio Call on the top right.*

2.19 Start Sharing Your Screen	This will allow you to **Share** your **Screen** with someone. **To Start Sharing Your Screen:** *Select the Contact* → *Select* *Start Sharing Your Screen on the top right.*

Section 3 - Edit Existing Message

This section will focus on changing the status of an existing message or **Deleting** an existing post.

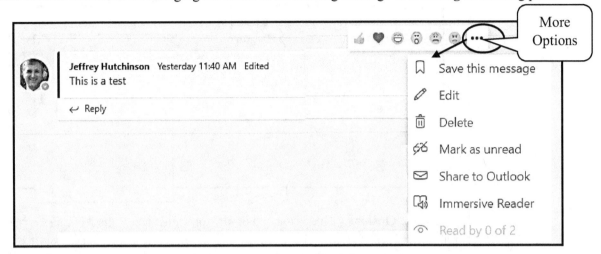

Concept	Explanation / *Command String in italic.*
2.20 Reply to Chat ↩ Reply	This will allow you to **Reply** to a **Conversation (Chat)**. **To Reply to a Conversation:** *Select* ↩ Reply *Reply below a message and enter the message.* 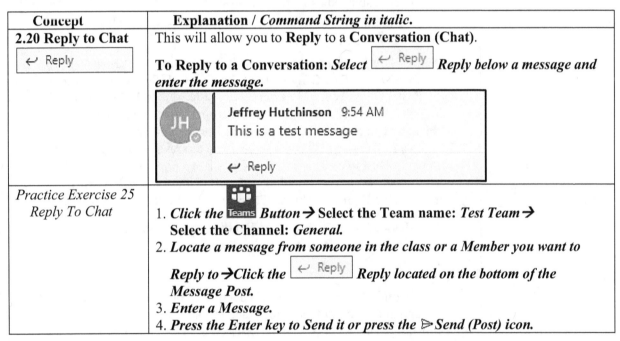
Practice Exercise 25 Reply To Chat	1. ***Click the*** [Teams] ***Button → Select the Team name: Test Team → Select the Channel: General.*** 2. ***Locate a message from someone in the class or a Member you want to Reply to → Click the*** ↩ Reply ***Reply located on the bottom of the Message Post.*** 3. ***Enter a Message.*** 4. ***Press the Enter key to Send it or press the ➢ Send (Post) icon.***

2.21 More Options ⋯	This will allow you to make changes to an existing **Message**. ⋯ **More options** are located on the top right side of the **Message Area**. ⋯ 🔖
	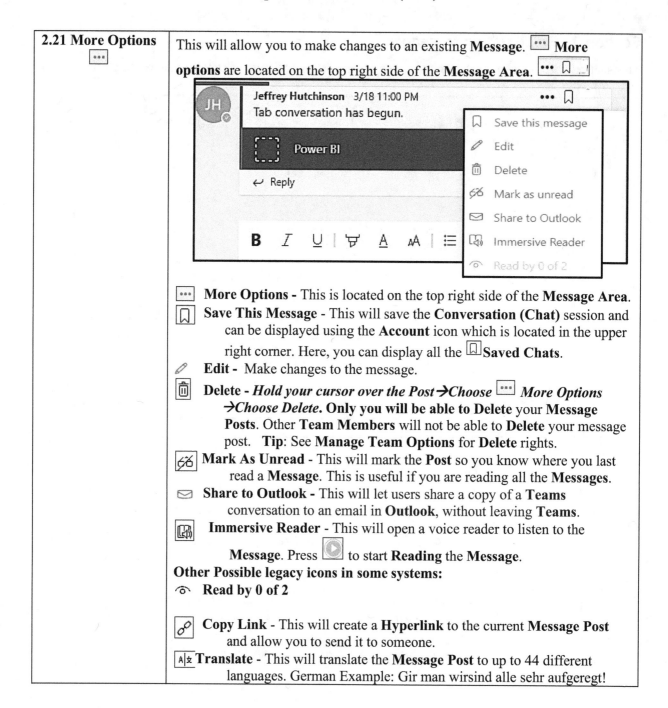

⋯ **More Options -** This is located on the top right side of the **Message Area**.

🔖 **Save This Message -** This will save the **Conversation (Chat)** session and can be displayed using the **Account** icon which is located in the upper right corner. Here, you can display all the 🔖**Saved Chats**.

✎ **Edit -** Make changes to the message.

🗑 **Delete -** *Hold your cursor over the Post→Choose* ⋯ *More Options →Choose Delete.* **Only you will be able to Delete** your **Message Posts.** Other **Team Members** will not be able to **Delete** your message post. **Tip:** See **Manage Team Options** for **Delete** rights.

🔖 **Mark As Unread -** This will mark the **Post** so you know where you last read a **Message**. This is useful if you are reading all the **Messages**.

✉ **Share to Outlook -** This will let users share a copy of a **Teams** conversation to an email in **Outlook**, without leaving **Teams**.

🔊 **Immersive Reader -** This will open a voice reader to listen to the **Message**. Press ▶ to start **Reading** the **Message**.

Other Possible legacy icons in some systems:

👁 **Read by 0 of 2**

🔗 **Copy Link -** This will create a **Hyperlink** to the current **Message Post** and allow you to send it to someone.

A⇄ **Translate -** This will translate the **Message Post** to up to 44 different languages. German Example: Gir man wirsind alle sehr aufgeregt!

Practice Exercise 26 *More Options*	1. ***Click the*** [Teams] ***Button → Select the Team name:*** *Test Team →* ***Select the Channel:*** *General.* 2. ***Select a Message Post →*** [...] ***More Options (located in the upper right corner of the Message area. →Test out the following options:*** 🗑 **Delete** - Try **Deleting** one of your **Message Posts.** ✉ **Mark As Unread** - Mark one of your **Message Posts** as **Unread** and review the results. 📖 **Immersive Reader** - Select a **Message Post** and choose this option to read the **Message Post** out loud. Click the ▶ **Button.** 🔖 **Save This Message** - **Save** one of your **Message Posts** to see if it will be listed under: 🟢 ***User Account →*** 🔖 ***Saved.*** **Tip:** The 🟢 User Account icon is located in the upper right corner of the interface. 3. ***Press the Enter key to Send it or press the*** ▷ ***Send (Post) icon.***
2.22 Status	The **Green Check Box** indicates you are available. The results will be displayed in the lower right corner of the **Account** icon. 🟢 Available 🔴 Busy ⛔ Do Not Disturb 🟡 Be Right Back ⚪ Appear Away Click on 🟢 🟢 Available 🔴 Busy ⛔ Do not disturb 🟡 Be right back ⚪ Appear away ↻ Reset status
Practice Exercise 27 *Status*	1. Change your **Status** by going to: 🟢 **User Account icon →** 📝 **Set Status Message.** 2. ***Review one of your Message Posts to see the change in Status.***

| **2.23 Command Bar** | If you are looking for a specific Conversation, you can search for it. The Search feature can be used to Search for people or specific topics of interest. Search is located on the top of the interface.
To Search: Enter a Keyword in the search box→ Press the Enter Key.

Type / or @ for a list of commands

The following special commands will provide additional capability:
/available - This sets your status to Available.
/away - This sets your status to Away.
/brb - This sets your status to Be Right Back.
/call - This will allow you to type a few letters of a name to **Call** them.
/dnd - This sets your status to Do Not Disturb.
/files - This displays your recent Files and allows you to open it.
/goto - This goes right to a Team or Channel.
    Tip: Keyboard command Ctrl G keys.
/help - This gets help with Teams in order to ask a question.
/keys - This displays the Keyboard Shortcuts.
/mentions - This will display all you're @mentions.
/saved - This will take you straight to your list of saved messages.
/unread - This will display all Unread Activities.
/whatsnew - This will display what's new in Teams.
/wiki - This adds a quick note.
@Praise - This shows gratitude for peers who went above and beyond.
@News - This will stay on top of the latest News.
@Places - This gets info about different Places.
@Stocks - This gets real-time Stock updates.
@Weather - This gets the latest Weather report.
@Wikipedia Search - This shares articles from Wikipedia.
More Apps - This adds additional Apps.
Tip: Keyboard command Ctrl E keys will place your cursor in the search box.
Navigation of the Left navigation panel:
  Activity Button - Ctrl 1 keys.
  Chat Button Ctrl 2 keys.
  Teams Button Ctrl 3 keys.
Emoji shortcuts in the Chat Message area.
  Type a colon ":" immediately followed by a word such as :frog :Happy
List of Shortcut keys- Ctrl . keys. |
| *Practice Exercise 28 Command Bar* | 1. ***Click the*** Teams ***Button →Select the Team name:*** *Test Team* →
Select the Channel: *General.*
2. *(Now that you have posted many messages, Search for a keyword such as Emoji).* Emoji
3. To find someone on the **Team** that knows something about **OneNote**:

/who   OneNote   > ×

  When you find an expert, you can add them to the **Conversation** and specify how much of the **Conversation** you want to **Share**.
4. Test the **/Goto** - This will list all available **Channels** for navigation. |

Student Project C	Have each student go to the **Team "Microsoft Team Class"** and enter random information about the **Channels** listed. For example, one student may have a conference or computer room that they can offer as a possible location. Another student may have a set of spare laptops that could be used for the physical class. Take a few minutes to allow the students to populate the **Conversation (Chat)** area and reply to other messages.

1. *Start a New Conversation but add a Subject by clicking on the* [A] *icon.*
2. *Enhance your message by using one of the following:*

    [📎] **Attach**   [☺] **Emoji**

    [GIF] **Giphy**   [😀] **Sticker**   [MEME] **Meme**

3. *Use as many tools to test the system such as:*

[A] **Format Controls**	[🔗] **Insert Link**
[B] **Bold**	[</>] **Code Snippet**
[I] **Italic**	[🗑] **Delete**
[U] **Underline**	[Paragraph ⌄] **Paragraph**
[🖊] **Text Highlighter Color**	[!] **Mark As Important**
[A] **Font Color**	[🗑] **Delete**
[AA] **Font Size**	[👁] **Mark As Unread**
[≔] **Bulleted List**	[📖] **Immersive Reader**
[≔] **Numbered List**	[🔖] **Save This Message**
[""] **Quote**	

4. *Go back to your post and edit it by clicking on the post→ More Options (located in the upper right corner of the Post→*[🖊]*Edit.*

Chapter 3 - Files

Files can be uploaded from several locations. The **Files** **Button** is located on the left side of the interface and the **Files Tab** is located on the top of the **Teams/Channel** area. The terms **Opened** and **Uploaded** have the same meaning because when a file is **Opened** it is essentially **Uploaded**.

Section 1 - Files Button

The **Files** **Button** is located on the left side of the interface and will display all files from different locations such as **Recent opened/uploaded**, **Microsoft Teams**, **Download** folder (located in the C: drive), and files located in **OneDrive** (see menu below).

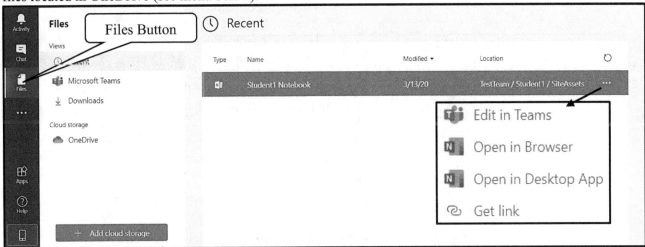

Concept	Explanation / *Command String in italic.*
3.1 Files	All **Files Uploaded** can be accessed by clicking the **Files** **Button** which is located on the left side of the interface (see the screen above). **Tip: Files** are physically stored in **Sharepoint** which allows them to be available for future access. **Tip:** Keyboard command **Ctrl** **6** keys.
3.2 Recent	This displays the **Recent** files that have been **Opened** and **Uploaded**. 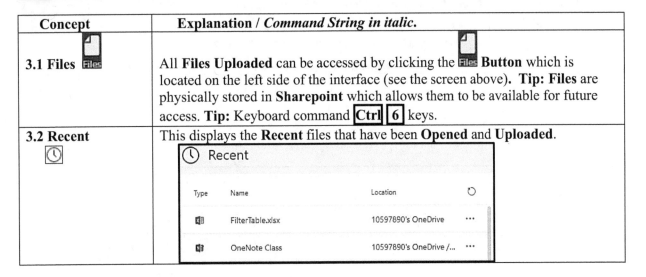

3.3 Microsoft Teams	This will list all files that have been **Uploaded** for all **Teams**. When you attach a file to a **Conversation (Chat)**, it is **Uploaded** to that **Channel** area. If you can't find the **Uploaded** file in the **Teams/Channel** Files **Tab**, then click on the Files **Button** to see all the files. When you select a file, the ⋯ **More Options** (located on the right side of the selected file) will allow you to **Edit In Teams, Open In Browser, Open In Desktop App, Download,** and **Get a Link**. 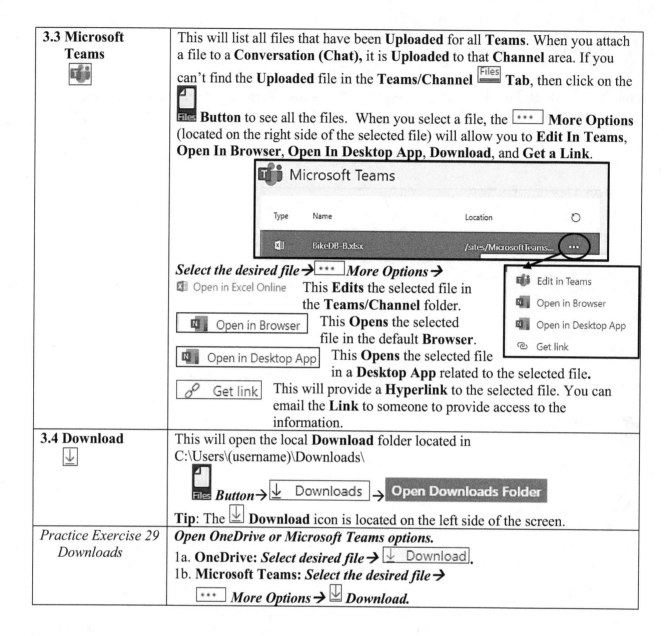 *Select the desired file →* ⋯ *More Options →* ⊠ Open in Excel Online This **Edits** the selected file in the **Teams/Channel** folder. ⊡ Open in Browser This **Opens** the selected file in the default **Browser**. ⊡ Open in Desktop App This **Opens** the selected file in a **Desktop App** related to the selected file. ⚯ Get link This will provide a **Hyperlink** to the selected file. You can email the **Link** to someone to provide access to the information.
3.4 Download ⤓	This will open the local **Download** folder located in C:\Users\(username)\Downloads\ Files *Button→* ⤓ Downloads → **Open Downloads Folder** **Tip**: The ⤓ **Download** icon is located on the left side of the screen.
Practice Exercise 29 Downloads	***Open OneDrive or Microsoft Teams options.*** 1a. **OneDrive:** *Select desired file →* ⤓ Download. 1b. **Microsoft Teams:** *Select the desired file →* ⋯ *More Options →* ⤓ *Download.*

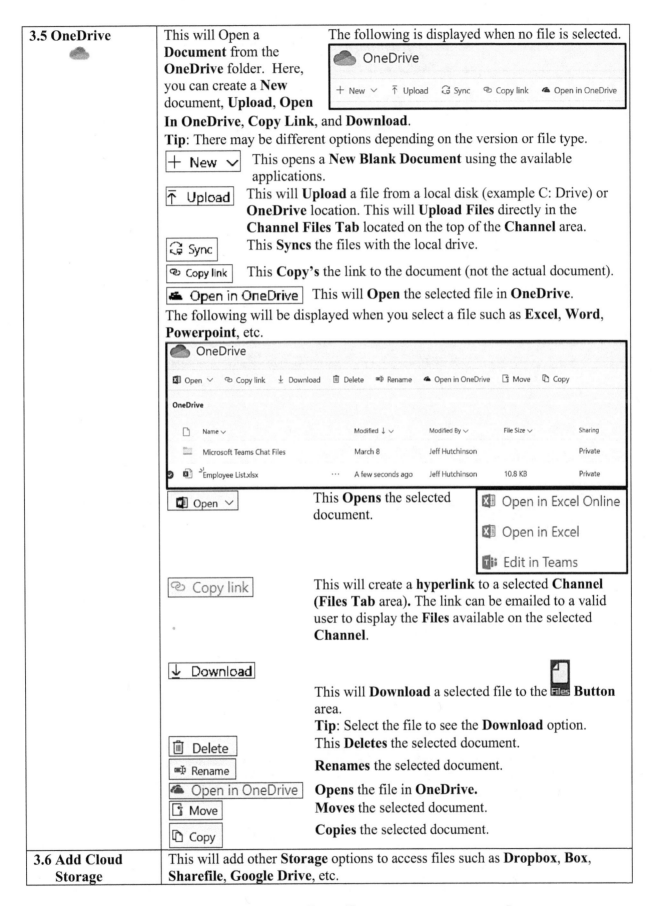

3.5 OneDrive	This will Open a **Document** from the **OneDrive** folder. Here, you can create a **New** document, **Upload**, **Open In OneDrive**, **Copy Link**, and **Download**. The following is displayed when no file is selected.

Tip: There may be different options depending on the version or file type.

+ New ˅ — This opens a **New Blank Document** using the available applications.

↑ Upload — This will **Upload** a file from a local disk (example C: Drive) or **OneDrive** location. This will **Upload Files** directly in the **Channel Files Tab** located on the top of the **Channel** area.

↻ Sync — This **Syncs** the files with the local drive.

Copy link — This **Copy's** the link to the document (not the actual document).

Open in OneDrive — This will **Open** the selected file in **OneDrive**.

The following will be displayed when you select a file such as **Excel**, **Word**, **Powerpoint**, etc.

Open ˅ — This **Opens** the selected document.
- Open in Excel Online
- Open in Excel
- Edit in Teams

Copy link — This will create a **hyperlink** to a selected **Channel (Files Tab** area**)**. The link can be emailed to a valid user to display the **Files** available on the selected **Channel**.

↓ Download — This will **Download** a selected file to the **Files Button** area.
Tip: Select the file to see the **Download** option.

🗑 Delete — This **Deletes** the selected document.

Rename — **Renames** the selected document.

Open in OneDrive — **Opens** the file in **OneDrive.**

Move — **Moves** the selected document.

Copy — **Copies** the selected document.

3.6 Add Cloud Storage	This will add other **Storage** options to access files such as **Dropbox, Box, Sharefile, Google Drive**, etc.

Click the following button + **Add cloud storage** →

Add cloud storage ×

Choose the cloud storage provider you'd like to use in Teams.

Dropbox
Dropbox simplifies the way teams work together with secure, easy-to-use collaboration tools and the fastest, most-reliable file sync platform.

Box
Box is a secure content management and collaboration platform helping teams and organizations easily share, manage, and collaborate on their most important information.

ShareFile
Citrix ShareFile helps people exchange files easily, securely, and professionally.

Google Drive
Get access to files anywhere through secure cloud storage and file backup for your photos, videos, files and more with Google Drive.

Section 2 - Files Tab In Teams (File Unselected)

The **Files** Tab is located at the top of the **Teams/Channels** area and will list files added to this **Channel**. When no files are highlighted (selected), you will be able to create a **New** document, **Upload** a file, **Get** a **Link** to the **Files Channel, Add Cloud Storage**, or **Open** the **Channel Files Tab** in **Sharepoint.** All **Files** added to a conversation can be found in the **Team Channel Files Tab**. This section will cover the options available when you first open the **Files Tab** or when no files are highlighted (selected).

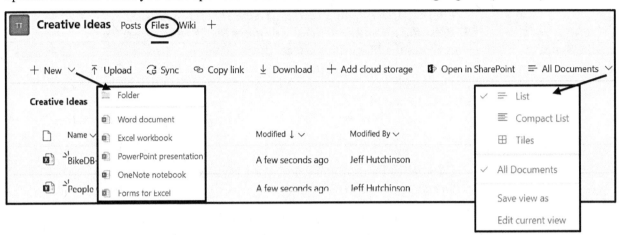

Concept	Explanation / *Command String in italic.*
3.7 Files	The **Files tab** can be accessed by clicking the desired **Channel** located on the top of the **Channels** area. You can then select the desired file. 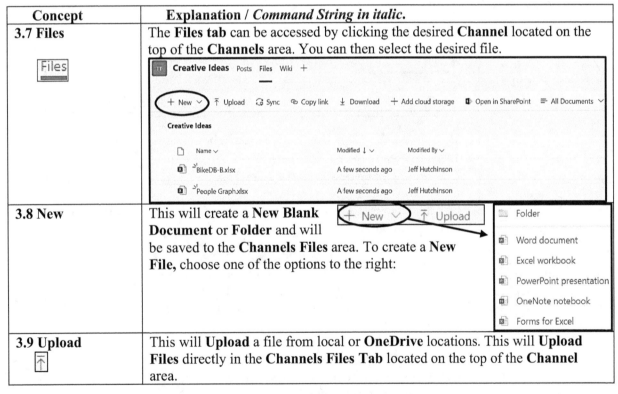
3.8 New	This will create a **New Blank Document** or **Folder** and will be saved to the **Channels Files** area. To create a **New File,** choose one of the options to the right:
3.9 Upload	This will **Upload** a file from local or **OneDrive** locations. This will **Upload Files** directly in the **Channels Files Tab** located on the top of the **Channel** area.

Practice Exercise 30 *Upload*	Add a new **Message Post** and **Upload** a file related to the **Message**. 1. *Click the* [Teams] *Button* →Select the Team name: *Test Team* → Select the Channel: *General*. 2. [A] *Format Control* →Enter the following message: Subject: *Upload File* Message: *Please refer to the attached file above.* File: ⌀ Attach Icon→C:\Data\Teams365-1\Teams1.jpg) 3. *Press the Enter key to Send it or press the* ▷ *Send (Post) icon.*
3.10 Sync	This **Syncs** the files with the local drive.
3.11 Copy Link	This will create a **hyperlink** to a selected **Channel (Files Tab** area). The link can be emailed to a valid user in order to display the **Files** available in a selected **Channel**. **Tip**: You can also **Copy** a **Link** to the **SharePoint** location which is the physical location for the files.
Practice Exercise 31 *Copy Link*	1. *Click the* [Teams] *Button* →Select the Team name: *Test Team* → Select the Channel: *General*. 2. *Files Tab (located on top next to the Channels Tab)* → [🔗] **Get Link**. **Get link** 📁 General Microsoft Teams SharePoint https://teams.microsoft.com/_#/school/files/General?threadId=19%3Adf935b7f000| 3. Press **Copy**. **Tip**: This feature used to be called **Get link**. 4. *Open a Browser and Paste the URL.* *This should navigate you to the Files Tab.*
3.12 Download	This will **Download** files.
3.13 Add Cloud Storage	This will add other **Storage** options to access files such as **Dropbox, Box, Sharefile, Google Drive**, etc. *Click the following button* [+ **Add cloud storage**]
3.14 Open In SharePoint	This will allow you to open a **File** stored in the **SharePoint** server. **Tip**: All files are physically stored in the **Sharepoint** server.
Student Project D *File Upload*	Pick a **File** that relates to the **Channel**, then enter a **Message** and **Upload** a **File**. 1. *Click the* [Teams] *Button* → Select the Team name: *Microsoft Teams Class* → Select the Channel: *General*. 2. *Start a New Conversation (Chat).* [A] *Format Control* → Subject: *Upload File* Message: *Please refer to the attached Files below.* ⌀ *Attach a file* →C:\Data\Teams365-1\Currency Rates.xlsx

	3. *Press the Enter key to Send it or press the* ▷ *Send (Post) icon.*
	Review the Files Tab to see if the file is listed.
	4. *Select the Files Tab→* 🔲 *Upload.*
	Upload the following files:
	      C:\Data\Teams365-1\People Graph.xlsx
	      C:\Data\Teams365-1\Presentation1 Student.pptx

Section 3 - Files Tab (Select File)

The 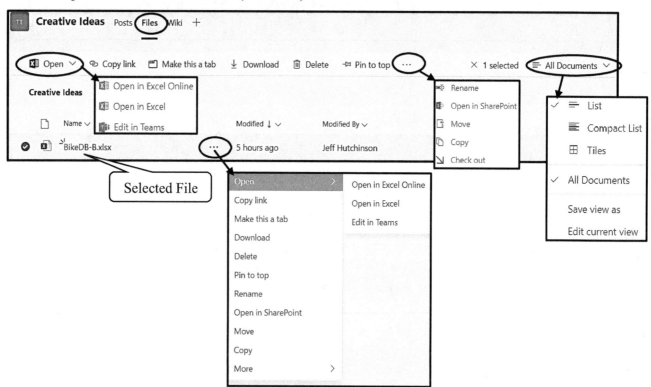 **Files Tab** is located at the top of the **Channels** and will list files added specifically to this **Channel**. When you highlight or select a file, the [•••] **More Options** will be available. This section will cover the options when a file is selected (see below).

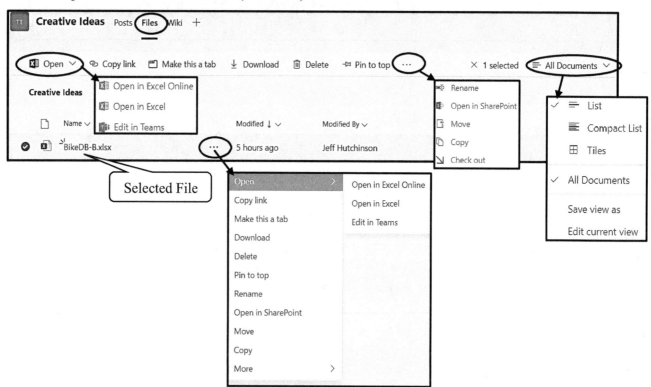

Concept	Explanation / *Command String in italic.*
3.15 Files Files	The **Files tab** can be accessed by clicking the desired **Channel** located on the top of the **Channels** area. Then select the desired file. 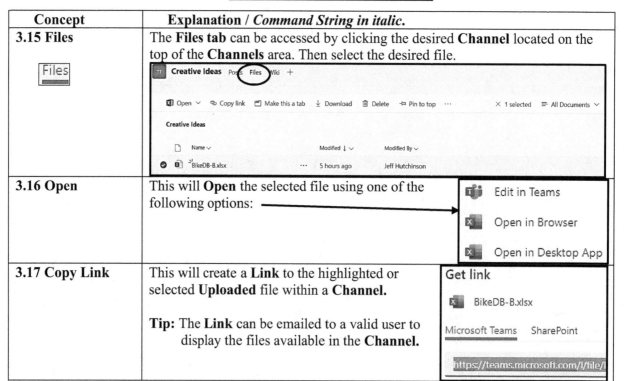
3.16 Open	This will **Open** the selected file using one of the following options: Edit in Teams Open in Browser Open in Desktop App
3.17 Copy Link	This will create a **Link** to the highlighted or selected **Uploaded** file within a **Channel.** **Tip:** The **Link** can be emailed to a valid user to display the files available in the **Channel.** Get link BikeDB-B.xlsx Microsoft Teams SharePoint https://teams.microsoft.com/l/file/

3.18 Make This A Tab	This will **Open** the selected file and place it next to the **Files Tab** (see below). 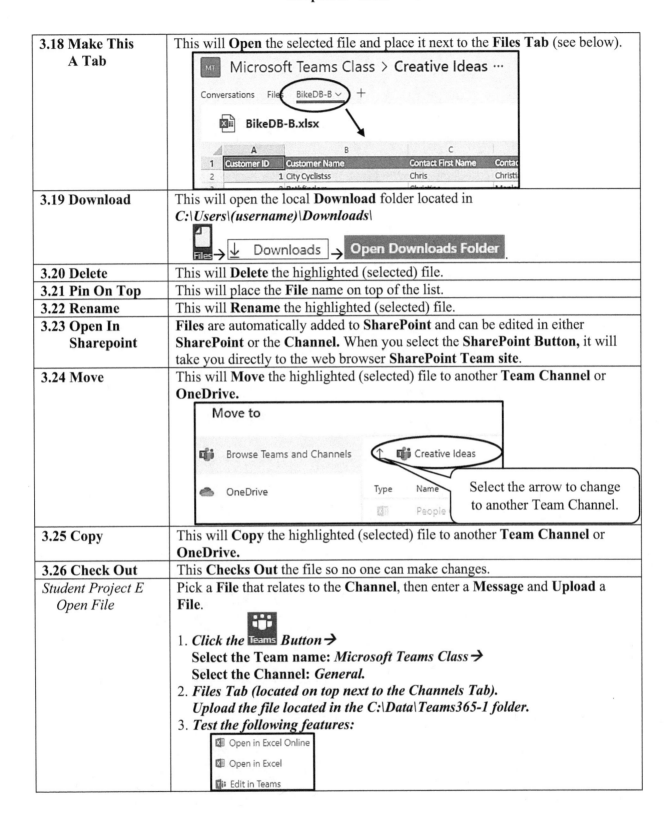
3.19 Download	This will open the local **Download** folder located in *C:\Users\(username)\Downloads*
3.20 Delete	This will **Delete** the highlighted (selected) file.
3.21 Pin On Top	This will place the **File** name on top of the list.
3.22 Rename	This will **Rename** the highlighted (selected) file.
3.23 Open In Sharepoint	**Files** are automatically added to **SharePoint** and can be edited in either **SharePoint** or the **Channel**. When you select the **SharePoint Button,** it will take you directly to the web browser **SharePoint Team site**.
3.24 Move	This will **Move** the highlighted (selected) file to another **Team Channel** or **OneDrive**.
3.25 Copy	This will **Copy** the highlighted (selected) file to another **Team Channel** or **OneDrive**.
3.26 Check Out	This **Checks Out** the file so no one can make changes.
Student Project E Open File	Pick a **File** that relates to the **Channel**, then enter a **Message** and **Upload** a **File**. 1. *Click the* Teams *Button→* *Select the Team name: Microsoft Teams Class→* *Select the Channel: General.* 2. *Files Tab (located on top next to the Channels Tab).* *Upload the file located in the C:\Data\Teams365-1 folder.* 3. *Test the following features:*

Chapter 4 - Activity

These are **Notifications** you may receive if someone adds you to a **Team,** someone starts a **New Chat** or a new **Team Member** is added to the **Team**. Also, to find specific information, you can **Filter** all **Messages** by Unread, Mentions, Replies, Following, Likes, Missed Calls, Voicemail, Apps, and Trending.

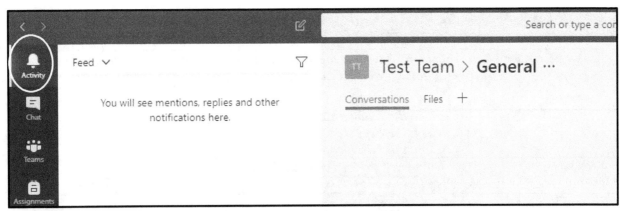

Concept	Explanation / *Command String in italic.*
4.1 Activity Button	Click on the Activity **Button** located on the left side of the interface to view your **Notifications**. **Tip**: Keyboard command Ctrl 1 **keys**.
4.2 Feed	These are comments or replies that other **Team Members** have made to a **Conversation (Chat)**. You will also get notified here if your name was applied to @**Mention** in any **Chat** session.
Practice Exercise 32 Activities	1. *Click the* Teams *Button →Select the Team name: Test Team →* ***Select the Channel: General.*** 2. *Start a new Massage and type in @(yourUserID).* 3. *Press the Enter key to Send it or press the ⊳ Send (Post) icon.* 4. *Review the results in the* Activity *Button.*
4.3 Team Activity	This shows all **Activity** in any of your **Teams**. When you click on one of the **Notifications,** it takes you to that particular **Conversation (Chat)**.
4.4 My Activity	This will show the **Activity** you have entered or posted.
Practice Exercise 33 Activities	*By now you should have many Messages in the Activity area.* 1. *Click on the* Activity *Button.* 2. *Click on the Activity to see the different Activity Messages.* 3. *Click on the Activity to Navigate you to the entry.*

4.5 Filter Icon	This will **Filter** your **Activities** and display the following information: Unread, Mentions, Replies, Likes, Missed call, Voicemail, Apps, Trending **Tip**: Click on the ▼ or ▽ **Filter** icon.
Practice Exercise 34 Filter	*If you do not have any messages in the Activity area, have another student post a Message in the Channel.* 1. *Click on the* Activity *Button.* 2. *Click on the Feed Tab.* 3. *Click on the Filter icon.*
4.6 Search	This will search any comment made in all **Teams**. Type / or @ for a list of commands
Student Project F Activity	1. *Click the* Teams *Button→ Select the Team name: Microsoft Team Class→ Create a new Channel:* ••• *More Options→* 🗒 *Add Channel→ MyNewChannel (initials)→* Create. 2. *Click the* Activity *Button.* 3. *Review The My Activity Tab.* 4. *Review The Feed Tab.* 5. *Filter to review the following:* Unread, Mentions, Replies

Chapter 5 - Video Meetings

This will allow you to schedule a **Meeting** with **Team Members**. You can also invite anyone outside of **Teams,** but you must log in to the **Teams Desktop** (in the future you will only need a browser and will log in as Anonymous). You can also schedule an **Audio**, **Video**, or **Screen Sharing** session. It integrates (syncs) with **Microsoft Outlook Calendar** so you won't have to keep track of multiple **Calendars**. Then, an email is sent to participants. However, they will need to accept the **Meeting** to update their **Calendars**.

Section 1 - Schedule A Meeting

This will cover the **Meeting** interface to **Schedule a Meeting.**

Press **Calendar** then, select **Schedule A Meeting** **Schedule a meeting** or **+ New meeting** **Button** to specify a specific date and time for the **Meeting**.

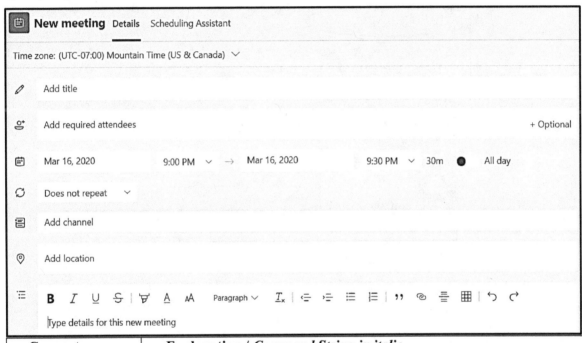

Concept	Explanation / *Command String in italic.*
5.1 Calendar Button **Calendar**	This is the button to click when you want to schedule a meeting. **Tip**: The button was previously called **Meetings** **Button.** **Tip**: Keyboard command **Ctrl** **4** keys.
5.2 Schedule A Meeting	This will arrange an online **Meeting** with co-workers. There are several ways to **Schedule A Meeting:** 1. **The Calendar Button:** **Calendar** **Button→** **+ New meeting**. 2. **Within A Chat Session:** **Chat** **Button→** or *Schedule A Meeting →* 3. **Within the Video Interface:** **Teams** **Button →** *Select a Team/Channel→* → **Schedule a meeting**

Practice Exercise 35
Schedule A
Meeting
	Schedule a **Meeting** to test out the **Meeting** features.
	
	1. **The Calendar Button:** Calendar *Button→* + New meeting.
	2. **Create a Meeting:**
	  Meeting Name: *Department Meeting*
	  Date: *Today*
	  Time: *Next half hour*
	  Add Required Attendees: *Invite one person*
	  Add Channel: *Creative Ideas*
	  Tip: You must invite someone or you won't be able to display the **Remote Meeting** capability.
	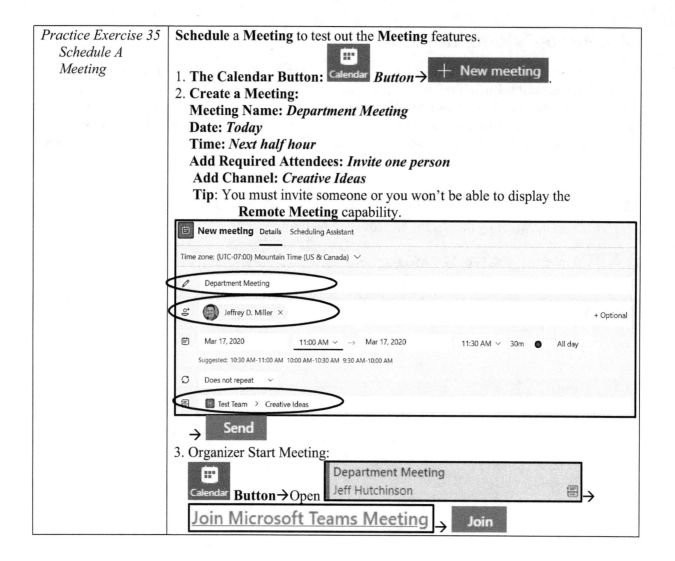
	  → Send
	3. Organizer Start Meeting:
	Calendar **Button**→Open Department Meeting / Jeff Hutchinson →
	Join Microsoft Teams Meeting → Join

Practice Exercise 36	**Schedule** a **Meeting** to test out the **Meeting** features.
	
	1. **The Calendar Button:** Calendar *Button→* + New meeting .
	2. **Create a Meeting:**
	  Meeting Name: *Group Meeting*
	  Date: *Today*
	  Time: *Two Hours from now*
	  Add Required Attendees: *Invite one person*
	    Tip: You must invite someone or you won't be able to display the **Remote Meeting** capability.
	
	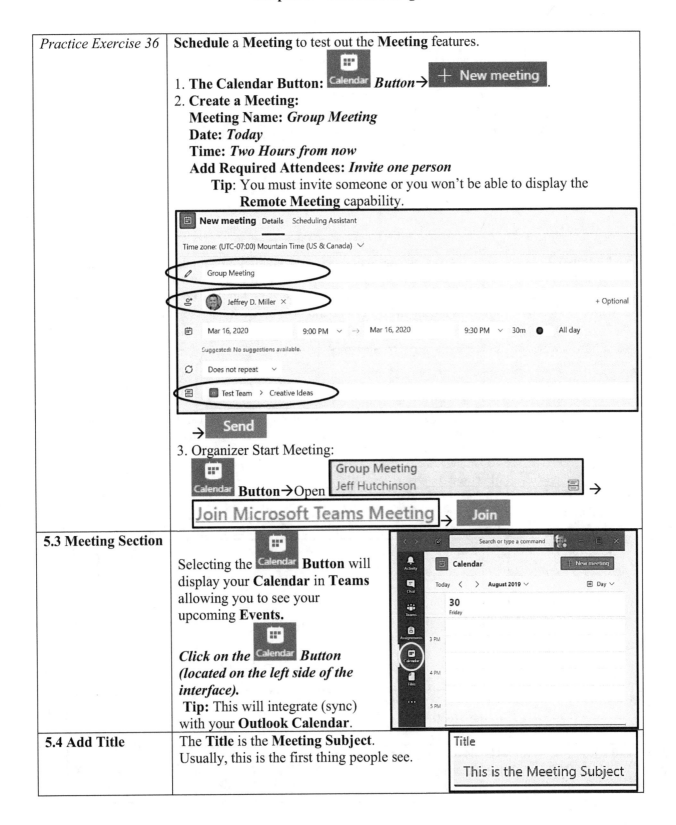
	
	3. Organizer Start Meeting:
	Calendar **Button**→Open Group Meeting / Jeff Hutchinson →
	Join Microsoft Teams Meeting → Join

5.3 Meeting Section	Selecting the Calendar **Button** will display your **Calendar** in **Teams** allowing you to see your upcoming **Events**. ***Click on the*** Calendar ***Button (located on the left side of the interface).*** **Tip:** This will integrate (sync) with your **Outlook Calendar**.
5.4 Add Title	The **Title** is the **Meeting Subject**. Usually, this is the first thing people see. Title This is the Meeting Subject

5.5 Add Required Attendees **Or Invite People**	This will allow you to **Invite** other **People** to the **Meeting**. *Type the first letter of the email address.* **Tip**: Preview other **Team** Members' status (**Busy** or **Available**) which is located under their **Picture Icon**.	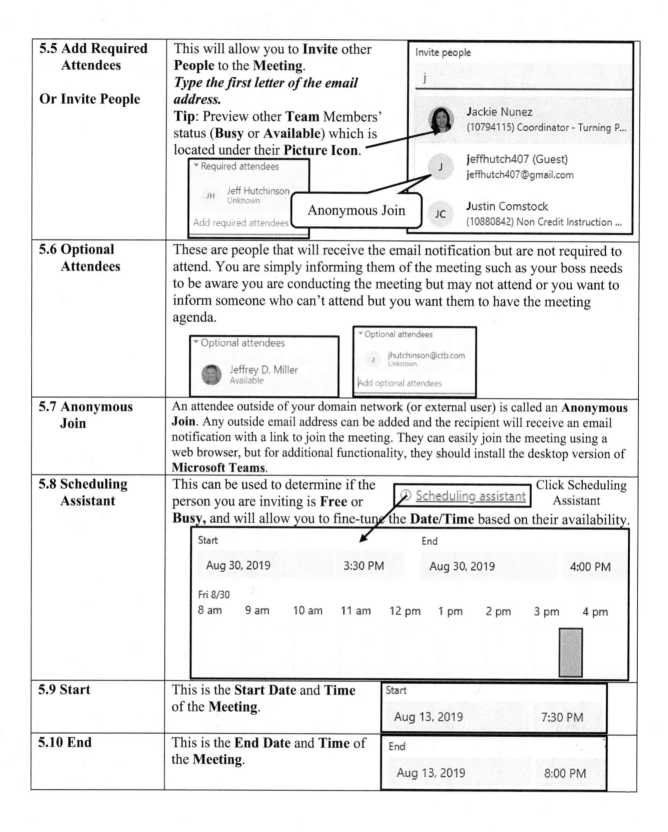
5.6 Optional Attendees	These are people that will receive the email notification but are not required to attend. You are simply informing them of the meeting such as your boss needs to be aware you are conducting the meeting but may not attend or you want to inform someone who can't attend but you want them to have the meeting agenda.	
5.7 Anonymous Join	An attendee outside of your domain network (or external user) is called an **Anonymous Join**. Any outside email address can be added and the recipient will receive an email notification with a link to join the meeting. They can easily join the meeting using a web browser, but for additional functionality, they should install the desktop version of **Microsoft Teams**.	
5.8 Scheduling Assistant	This can be used to determine if the person you are inviting is **Free** or **Busy**, and will allow you to fine-tune the **Date/Time** based on their availability. Click Scheduling Assistant	
5.9 Start	This is the **Start Date** and **Time** of the **Meeting**.	Start Aug 13, 2019 7:30 PM
5.10 End	This is the **End Date** and **Time** of the **Meeting**.	End Aug 13, 2019 8:00 PM

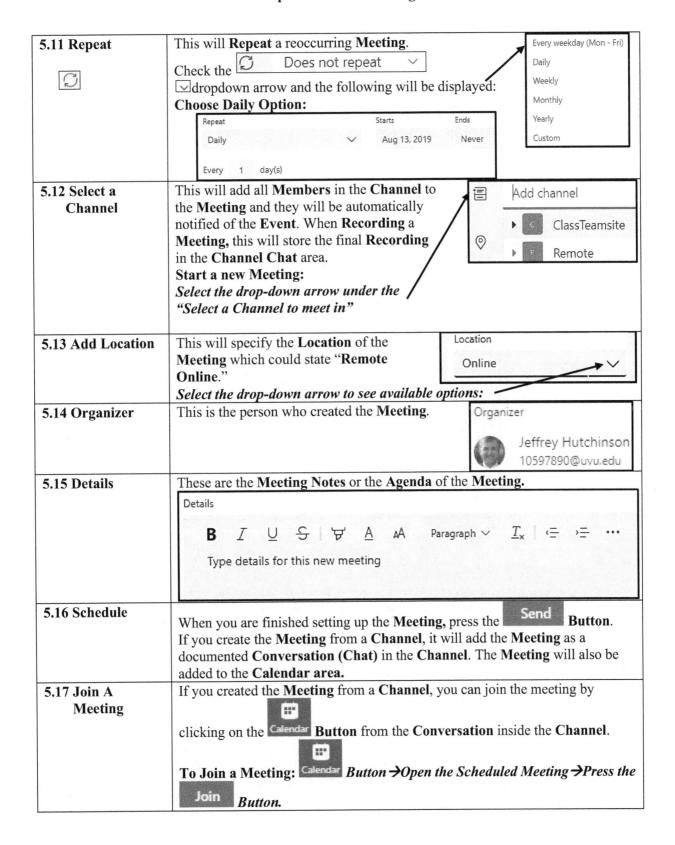

5.11 Repeat	This will **Repeat** a reoccurring **Meeting**. Check the [Does not repeat ∨] dropdown arrow and the following will be displayed: **Choose Daily Option:**
5.12 Select a Channel	This will add all **Members** in the **Channel** to the **Meeting** and they will be automatically notified of the **Event**. When **Recording** a **Meeting,** this will store the final **Recording** in the **Channel Chat** area. **Start a new Meeting:** *Select the drop-down arrow under the "Select a Channel to meet in"*
5.13 Add Location	This will specify the **Location** of the **Meeting** which could state "**Remote Online."** *Select the drop-down arrow to see available options:*
5.14 Organizer	This is the person who created the **Meeting**.
5.15 Details	These are the **Meeting Notes** or the **Agenda** of the **Meeting**.
5.16 Schedule	When you are finished setting up the **Meeting**, press the **Send** Button. If you create the **Meeting** from a **Channel**, it will add the **Meeting** as a documented **Conversation (Chat)** in the **Channel**. The **Meeting** will also be added to the **Calendar area.**
5.17 Join A Meeting	If you created the **Meeting** from a **Channel**, you can join the meeting by clicking on the **Calendar** Button from the **Conversation** inside the **Channel**. **To Join a Meeting:** **Calendar** *Button →Open the Scheduled Meeting →Press the* **Join** *Button.*

Student Project G Select A Channel	**Schedule** a **Meeting** to test out the **Meeting** features.

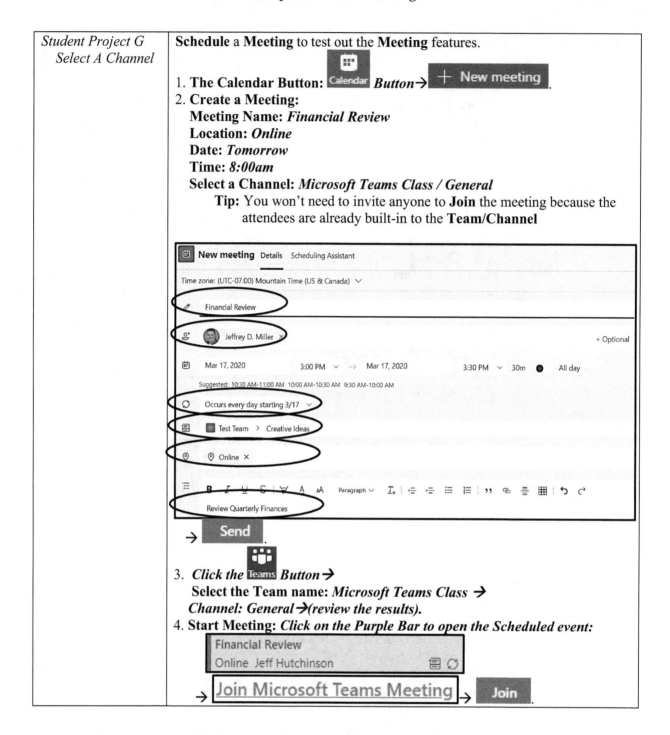

1. **The Calendar Button:** [Calendar] *Button→* [+ New meeting].
2. **Create a Meeting:**
   Meeting Name: *Financial Review*
   Location: *Online*
   Date: *Tomorrow*
   Time: *8:00am*
   Select a Channel: *Microsoft Teams Class / General*
   > **Tip:** You won't need to invite anyone to **Join** the meeting because the attendees are already built-in to the **Team/Channel**

New meeting Details Scheduling Assistant

Time zone: (UTC-07:00) Mountain Time (US & Canada) ⌄

Financial Review

Jeffrey D. Miller ✕   + Optional

Mar 17, 2020   3:00 PM ⌄ → Mar 17, 2020   3:30 PM ⌄ 30m ⬤ All day
Suggested: 10:30 AM-11:00 AM 10:00 AM-10:30 AM 9:30 AM-10:00 AM

Occurs every day starting 3/17 ⌄

Test Team > Creative Ideas

Online ✕

Review Quarterly Finances

→ [Send].

3. *Click the* [Teams] *Button→*
   Select the Team name: *Microsoft Teams Class →*
   Channel: *General →(review the results).*
4. **Start Meeting:** *Click on the Purple Bar to open the Scheduled event:*

   Financial Review
   Online Jeff Hutchinson

   → Join Microsoft Teams Meeting → [Join].

5.18 New Live Event	A **Team Event** can hold up to 10,000 participants in real-time. You have more control over **Video**, audience interaction, and reporting.
	Live Event Permissions:
	  People and Groups - You will need to specify the specific people that will attend the event.
	  Org-Wide - Anyone in your organization can attend the event.
	  Public - The event is open to everyone.
	How will you produce your live event? Teams:
	  ☐ **Record (available to producers and presenters.)**
	  ☑ **Recording (available to attendees.)**
	  ☐ **Captions (preview)**
	  ☑ **Attendee (Engagement Report.)**
	  ☐ **Q&A**
	Tip: For large **Events,** you may need the following people to help:
	  1 - **Producer** - Their role is to make sure **Audio** and **Video** are working properly and notify you immediately if something is wrong.
	  2. **Q&A Moderator** - They will review **Questions** and either **Answer** them online or summarize them for a review during the **Q&A** session at the end of the **Event**.

Practice Exercise 37	**To create a new Live Event:** 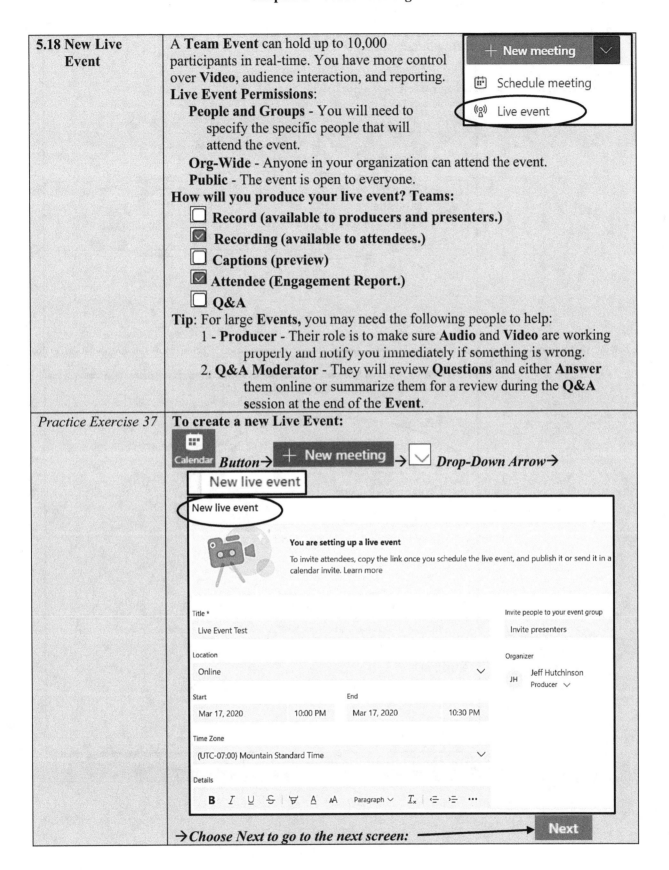 →*Choose Next to go to the next screen:*

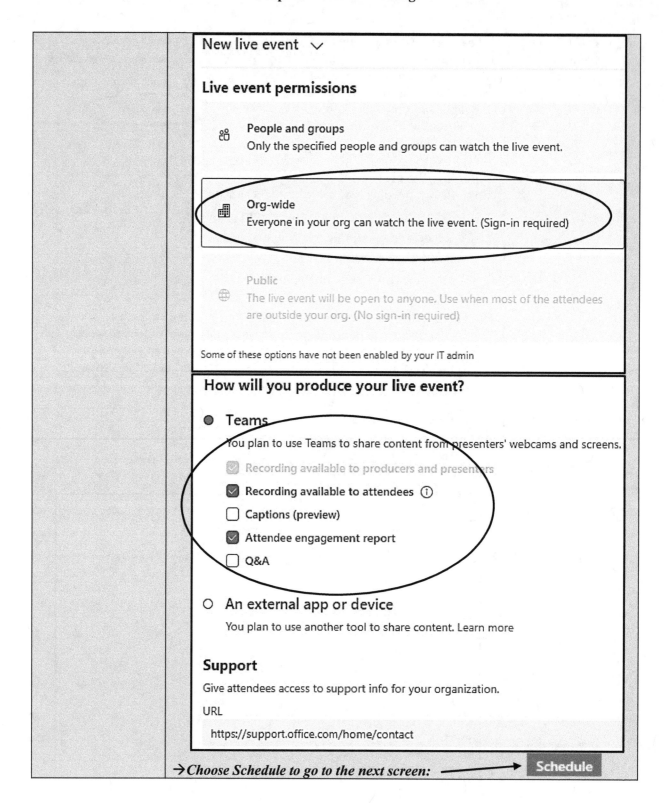

New live event ⌄

Live event permissions

⌘ People and groups
   Only the specified people and groups can watch the live event.

⊞ Org-wide
   Everyone in your org can watch the live event. (Sign-in required)

⊕ Public
   The live event will be open to anyone. Use when most of the attendees
   are outside your org. (No sign-in required)

Some of these options have not been enabled by your IT admin

How will you produce your live event?

⦿ Teams
   You plan to use Teams to share content from presenters' webcams and screens.

   ☑ Recording available to producers and presenters
   ☑ Recording available to attendees ⓘ
   ☐ Captions (preview)
   ☑ Attendee engagement report
   ☐ Q&A

○ **An external app or device**
   You plan to use another tool to share content. Learn more

Support

Give attendees access to support info for your organization.
URL

https://support.office.com/home/contact

→ *Choose Schedule to go to the next screen:* ——→ Schedule

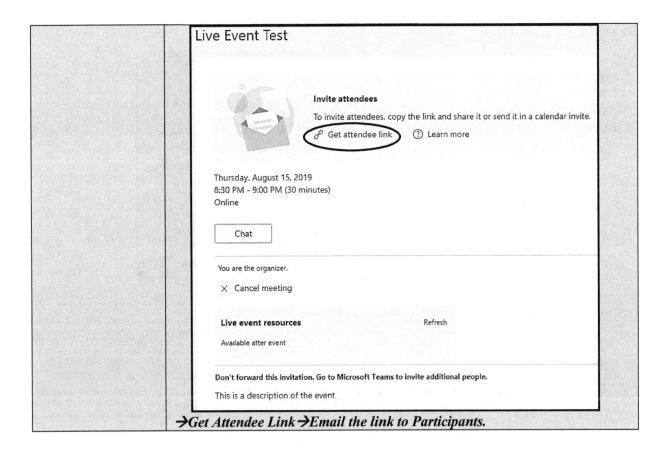

→*Get Attendee Link→Email the link to Participants.*

Section 2 - Video Call

This is **Microsoft's Video Conferencing** system that allows you to connect with remote **Members** in your **Team** or **Company**.

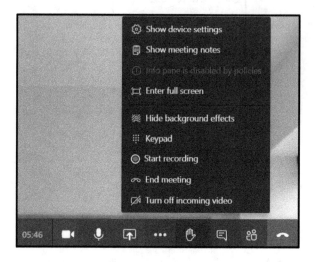

Concept	Explanation / *Command String in italic.*

5.19 Start Video Call
 	
 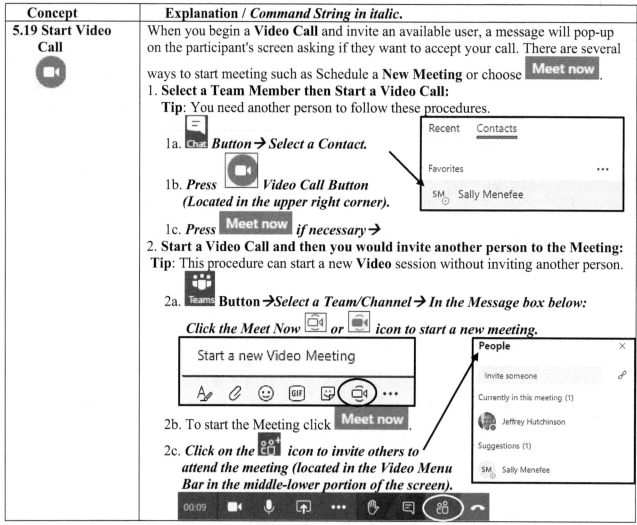
	When you begin a **Video Call** and invite an available user, a message will pop-up on the participant's screen asking if they want to accept your call. There are several ways to start meeting such as Schedule a **New Meeting** or choose **Meet now**.
	 1. Select a Team Member then Start a Video Call:
	   Tip: You need another person to follow these procedures.
	
	   1a. **Chat** *Button→ Select a Contact.*
	
	   1b. *Press* **Video Call Button** *(Located in the upper right corner).*
	
	   1c. *Press* **Meet now** *if necessary→*
	 2. Start a Video Call and then you would invite another person to the Meeting:
	  Tip: This procedure can start a new **Video** session without inviting another person.
	
	   2a. **Teams** *Button→Select a Team/Channel→ In the Message box below:*
	   Click the Meet Now or icon to start a new meeting.
	
	   2b. To start the Meeting click **Meet now**.
	
	   2c. *Click on the icon to invite others to attend the meeting (located in the Video Menu Bar in the middle-lower portion of the screen).*

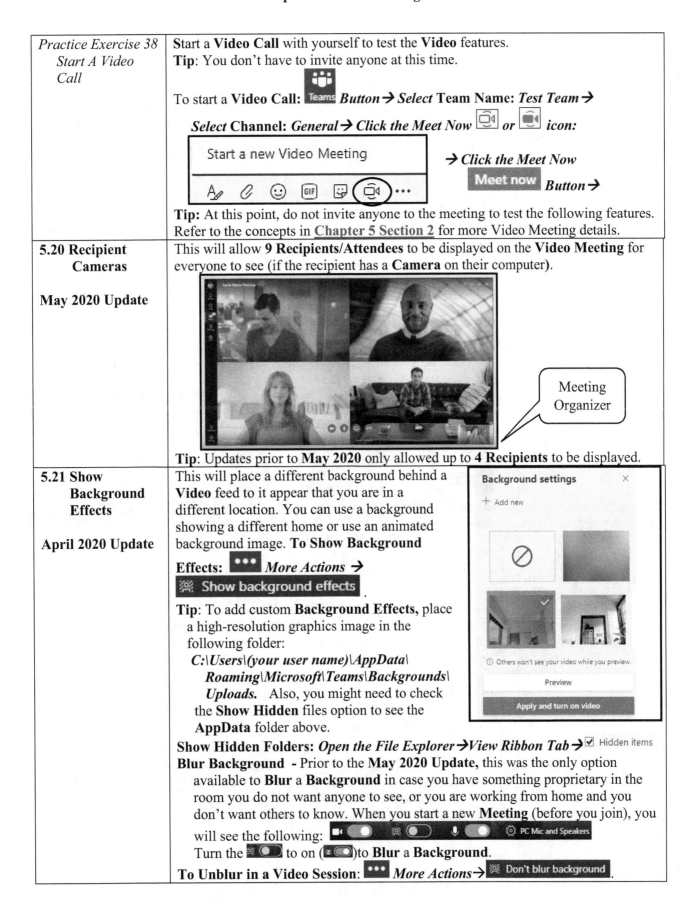

Practice Exercise 38 *Start A Video* *Call*	Start a **Video Call** with yourself to test the **Video** features. **Tip**: You don't have to invite anyone at this time. To start a **Video Call:** [Teams] *Button→ Select* **Team Name:** *Test Team →* *Select* **Channel:** *General→ Click the Meet Now* 🎥 *or* 🎥 *icon:* Start a new Video Meeting → *Click the Meet Now* [Aⱽ] [🖉] [☺] [GIF] [😊] [🎥] ••• **Meet now** *Button→* **Tip:** At this point, do not invite anyone to the meeting to test the following features. Refer to the concepts in <u>Chapter 5 Section 2</u> for more Video Meeting details.
5.20 Recipient **Cameras** **May 2020 Update**	This will allow **9 Recipients/Attendees** to be displayed on the **Video Meeting** for everyone to see (if the recipient has a **Camera** on their computer). Meeting Organizer **Tip:** Updates prior to **May 2020** only allowed up to **4 Recipients** to be displayed.
5.21 Show **Background** **Effects** **April 2020 Update**	This will place a different background behind a **Video** feed to it appear that you are in a different location. You can use a background showing a different home or use an animated background image. **To Show Background** Effects: ••• *More Actions →* [📷 **Show background effects**]. **Background settings** × + Add new ⊘ ✓ ⓘ Others won't see your video while you preview. Preview Apply and turn on video **Tip:** To add custom **Background Effects,** place a high-resolution graphics image in the following folder: *C:\Users\(your user name)\AppData\Roaming\Microsoft\Teams\Backgrounds\Uploads.* Also, you might need to check the **Show Hidden** files option to see the **AppData** folder above. **Show Hidden Folders:** *Open the File Explorer→View Ribbon Tab →* ☑ Hidden items **Blur Background** - Prior to the **May 2020 Update,** this was the only option available to **Blur** a **Background** in case you have something proprietary in the room you do not want anyone to see, or you are working from home and you don't want others to know. When you start a new **Meeting** (before you join), you will see the following: [🎥 ⚪] [📷 ⚪] [🎙 ⚪] [⚙ PC Mic and Speakers] Turn the [📷 ⚪] to on ([📷⚫])to **Blur** a **Background.** **To Unblur in a Video Session:** ••• *More Actions→* [📷 Don't blur background].

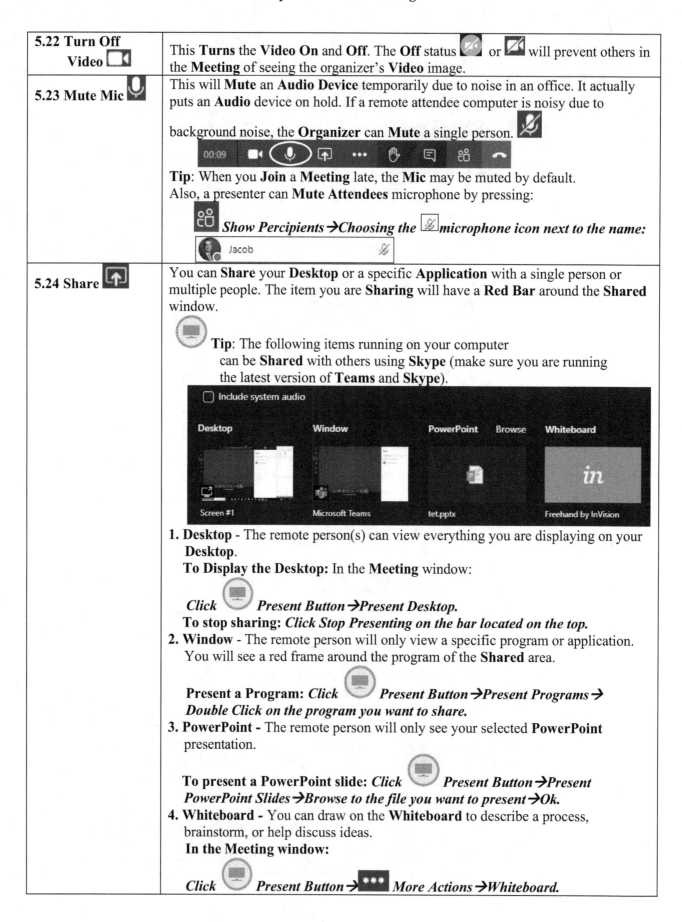

5.22 Turn Off Video	This **Turns** the **Video On** and **Off**. The **Off** status or will prevent others in the **Meeting** of seeing the organizer's **Video** image.
5.23 Mute Mic	This will **Mute** an **Audio Device** temporarily due to noise in an office. It actually puts an **Audio** device on hold. If a remote attendee computer is noisy due to background noise, the **Organizer** can **Mute** a single person. 00:09 **Tip**: When you **Join** a **Meeting** late, the **Mic** may be muted by default. Also, a presenter can **Mute Attendees** microphone by pressing: *Show Percipients→Choosing the microphone icon next to the name:* Jacob
5.24 Share	You can **Share** your **Desktop** or a specific **Application** with a single person or multiple people. The item you are **Sharing** will have a **Red Bar** around the **Shared** window. **Tip**: The following items running on your computer can be **Shared** with others using **Skype** (make sure you are running the latest version of **Teams** and **Skype**). Include system audio Desktop Window PowerPoint Browse Whiteboard Screen #1 Microsoft Teams tet.pptx Freehand by InVision 1. **Desktop** - The remote person(s) can view everything you are displaying on your **Desktop**. **To Display the Desktop**: In the **Meeting** window: *Click Present Button→Present Desktop.* **To stop sharing**: *Click Stop Presenting on the bar located on the top.* 2. **Window** - The remote person will only view a specific program or application. You will see a red frame around the program of the **Shared** area. **Present a Program**: *Click Present Button→Present Programs→ Double Click on the program you want to share.* 3. **PowerPoint** - The remote person will only see your selected **PowerPoint** presentation. **To present a PowerPoint slide**: *Click Present Button→Present PowerPoint Slides→Browse to the file you want to present→Ok.* 4. **Whiteboard** - You can draw on the **Whiteboard** to describe a process, brainstorm, or help discuss ideas. **In the Meeting window**: *Click Present Button→ More Actions→Whiteboard.*

5.25 Take Control	A participant can take control and become a presenter as long as they have released the sharing or **Unsharing** the controls. If the presenter is **Sharing** their screen, they can release the controls by clicking the ⬇ **Release Sharing** your screen. If the **Share** button shows an ⬆ up arrow, then the original presenter is **Sharing** their screen and the controls cannot be transferred to a participant.
5.26 Show Conversation 💬	This will display a **Meeting Conversation (Chat)** screen on the right side of the interface. It will be viewable by everyone in the **Meeting**. 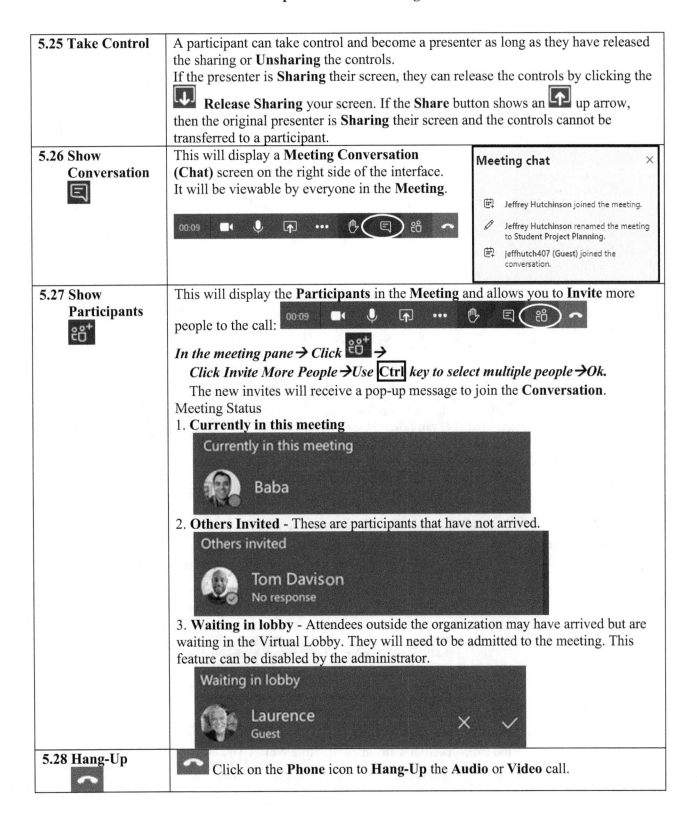
5.27 Show Participants	This will display the **Participants** in the **Meeting** and allows you to **Invite** more people to the call: *In the meeting pane → Click* → *Click Invite More People → Use* Ctrl *key to select multiple people → Ok.* The new invites will receive a pop-up message to join the **Conversation.** Meeting Status 1. **Currently in this meeting** Currently in this meeting Baba 2. **Others Invited** - These are participants that have not arrived. Others invited Tom Davison No response 3. **Waiting in lobby** - Attendees outside the organization may have arrived but are waiting in the Virtual Lobby. They will need to be admitted to the meeting. This feature can be disabled by the administrator. Waiting in lobby Laurence Guest ✕ ✓
5.28 Hang-Up 📞	📞 Click on the **Phone** icon to **Hang-Up** the **Audio** or **Video** call.

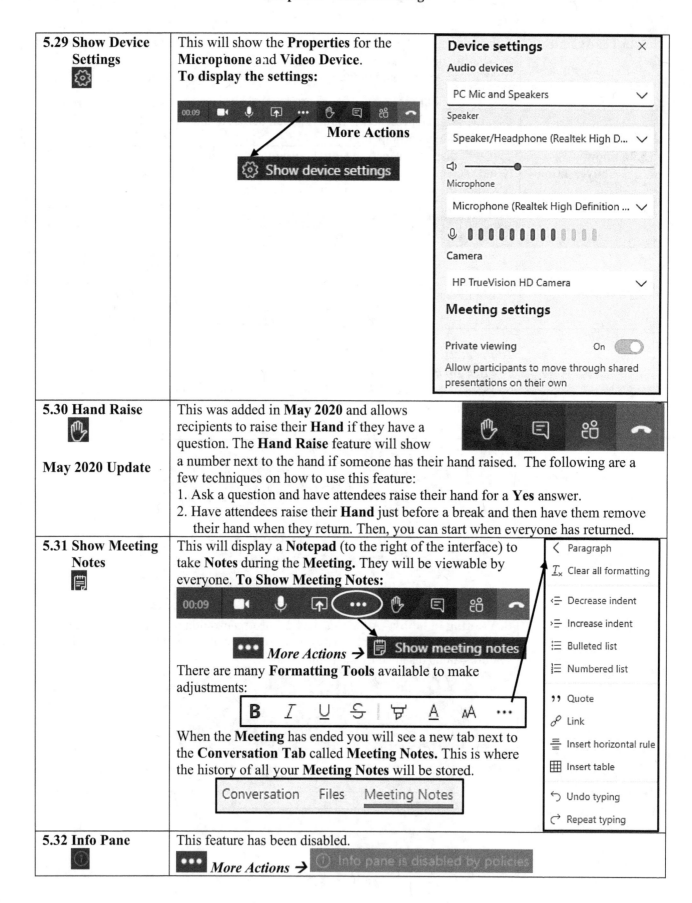

5.29 Show Device Settings ⚙	This will show the **Properties** for the **Microphone** and **Video Device**. **To display the settings:**
5.30 Hand Raise ✋ **May 2020 Update**	This was added in **May 2020** and allows recipients to raise their **Hand** if they have a question. The **Hand Raise** feature will show a number next to the hand if someone has their hand raised. The following are a few techniques on how to use this feature: 1. Ask a question and have attendees raise their hand for a **Yes** answer. 2. Have attendees raise their **Hand** just before a break and then have them remove their hand when they return. Then, you can start when everyone has returned.
5.31 Show Meeting Notes	This will display a **Notepad** (to the right of the interface) to take **Notes** during the **Meeting.** They will be viewable by everyone. **To Show Meeting Notes:** There are many **Formatting Tools** available to make adjustments: When the **Meeting** has ended you will see a new tab next to the **Conversation Tab** called **Meeting Notes.** This is where the history of all your **Meeting Notes** will be stored.
5.32 Info Pane ⓘ	This feature has been disabled.

More Actions

⚙ Show device settings

Device settings ✕
Audio devices
PC Mic and Speakers ⌄
Speaker
Speaker/Headphone (Realtek High D... ⌄
◀) —————●——————
Microphone
Microphone (Realtek High Definition ... ⌄
🎤 ▮▮▮▮▮▮▮▮▮▯▯▯
Camera
HP TrueVision HD Camera ⌄
Meeting settings
Private viewing   On ⬤
Allow participants to move through shared presentations on their own

⋯ More Actions → 🗒 Show meeting notes

B *I* U S̶ ✐ A A̲A ⋯

Conversation   Files   Meeting Notes

‹ Paragraph
Tₓ Clear all formatting
⮌ Decrease indent
⮞ Increase indent
☰ Bulleted list
☰ Numbered list
,, Quote
🔗 Link
☰ Insert horizontal rule
⊞ Insert table
↺ Undo typing
↻ Repeat typing

⋯ More Actions → ⓘ Info pane is disabled by policies

5.33 Enter Full Screen 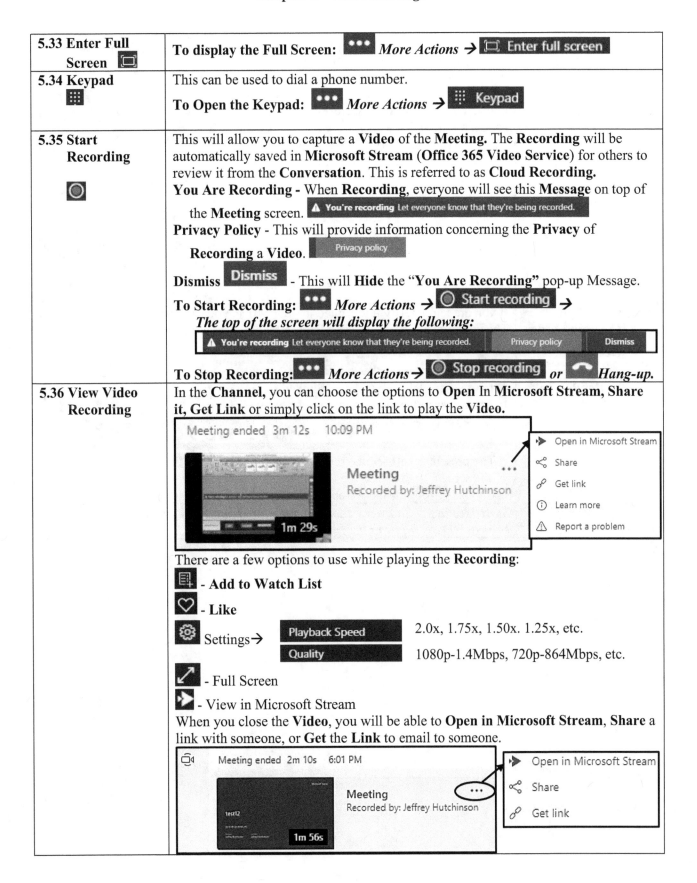	To display the Full Screen: ●●● *More Actions* → ⬚ Enter full screen
5.34 Keypad ▦	This can be used to dial a phone number. **To Open the Keypad:** ●●● *More Actions* → ▦ Keypad
5.35 Start Recording ⦿	This will allow you to capture a **Video** of the **Meeting**. The **Recording** will be automatically saved in **Microsoft Stream (Office 365 Video Service)** for others to review it from the **Conversation**. This is referred to as **Cloud Recording**. **You Are Recording** - When **Recording**, everyone will see this **Message** on top of the **Meeting** screen. ⚠ **You're recording** Let everyone know that they're being recorded. **Privacy Policy** - This will provide information concerning the **Privacy** of **Recording** a Video. Privacy policy **Dismiss** Dismiss - This will **Hide** the "**You Are Recording**" pop-up Message. **To Start Recording:** ●●● *More Actions* → ⦿ Start recording → *The top of the screen will display the following:* ⚠ **You're recording** Let everyone know that they're being recorded. Privacy policy Dismiss **To Stop Recording:** ●●● *More Actions* → ⦿ Stop recording *or* ☎ *Hang-up.*
5.36 View Video Recording	In the **Channel,** you can choose the options to **Open In Microsoft Stream, Share** it, **Get Link** or simply click on the link to play the **Video.**

There are a few options to use while playing the **Recording**:

⊞ - **Add to Watch List**

♡ - **Like**

⚙ Settings→ | Playback Speed | 2.0x, 1.75x, 1.50x. 1.25x, etc.
| Quality | 1080p-1.4Mbps, 720p-864Mbps, etc.

⬈ - Full Screen

▶ - View in Microsoft Stream

When you close the **Video**, you will be able to **Open in Microsoft Stream**, **Share** a link with someone, or **Get** the **Link** to email to someone.

5.37 Mute Attendees	If an attendee comes from a noisy environment, the **Organizer** can **Mute** them as needed. By default, late attendees will be **Muted** when they arrive. If someone has been **Muted,** they will be notified but can **Unmute** themselves if they have a question. To **Mute** everyone, choose the **Mute All** button. Everyone will get a notification and be able to **Unmute** themselves if necessary.
5.38 Turn Off Incoming Video	If you are temporarily interrupted in your office, you can turn off your **Video Feed**. This will prevent others in the **Meeting Room** from seeing you. **To Turn Off Incoming Video:** ●●● *More Actions →* ⊠ Turn off incoming video
5.39 Attendee Take Control	**Attendees** can take control of a **Shared** session. 1. **Attendees** will need to request control by clicking the following: Give Control. Give control ∨ ⊠ Stop presenting ↺ 2. The presenter will see the request of Allow / Deny located on the top of the screen. Choose Allow for the **Attendee** to take control of the session.
Practice Exercise 39	***Start Meeting→ Share my Desktop→Remote attendee requests to take control→Press Allow to accept the request.***

Student Project H	**Schedule** a **Meeting** with another person to test out the **Meeting** features. **Tip**: You need another person to follow these procedures. 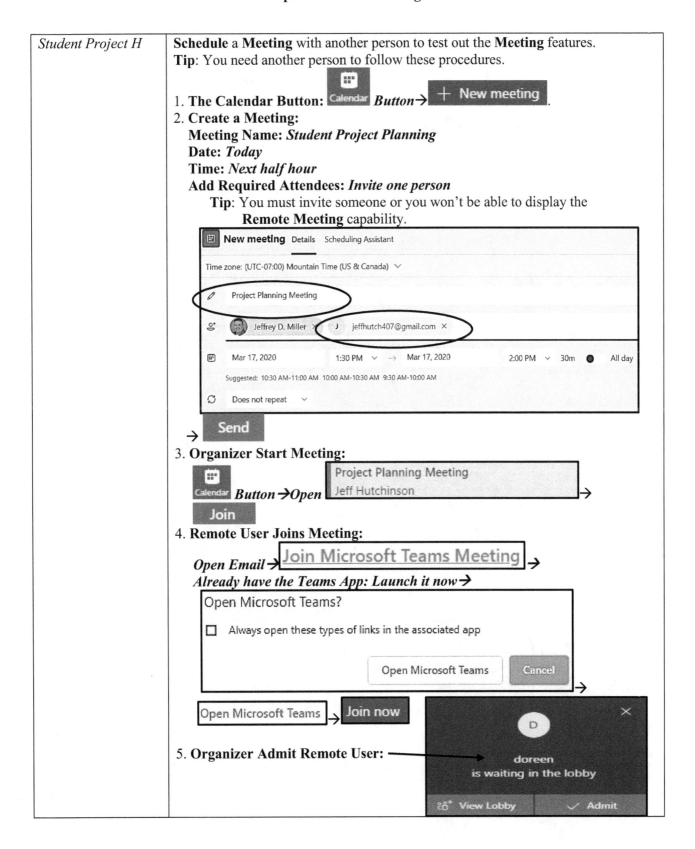

5.40 Video Call From A Team	Another way to start a **Video Call** is from the **Team**. Each **Team** will have members assigned. When a meeting is started in the **Chat** line, all members will be assigned to the **New Meeting**. If you choose [Meet now], all **Members** of the **Team** will be notified (if they are currently at their computers) to connect to the **Video Call**.

Practice Exercise 40	1. *Click the* [Teams] *Button* → *Select the Team name:* *Test Team* →
	2. **Verify that members have been added to team:**
	   Select the Test Team →*Next to the "Test Team" name* →
	   Click the More Options [•••] → ***Choose Manage Members***
	3. ***Start the Video Call: Select the General Channel*** → [camera] → [Meet now].
	
	This Team is set up to test the Teams features. The Team is the Project and the Channels are the tasks to be performed.
	
	A̶ 🖉 ☺ [GIF] 🗺 📹 ••• ▷

5.41 Pop-out Boxes **May 2020 Update**	You can now create **Pop-out boxes** for different **Chats** going on at the same time.

Section 3 - Homework Assignment

Concept	Explanation / *Command String in italic.*
Student Project I *Student Meetings*	After class (or during class depending on time), choose a partner and test out the **Video Meeting** capability. 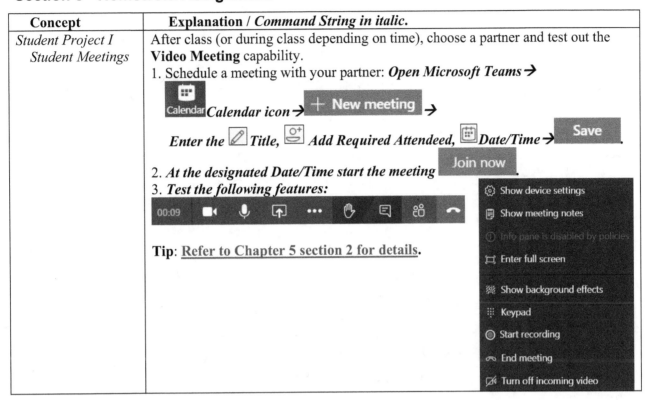

Chapter 6 - Phone Calls (Optional)

Audio Calls can be integrated with a **Phone PBX** system and will allow you to call anyone in the world through the **Teams** interface. You will be able to see missed calls, leave a voicemail, or transfer calls automatically. But it also supports call queues to hold multiple inbound calls. This capability is usually not available, however, if it is, the following are features you will need to test out:

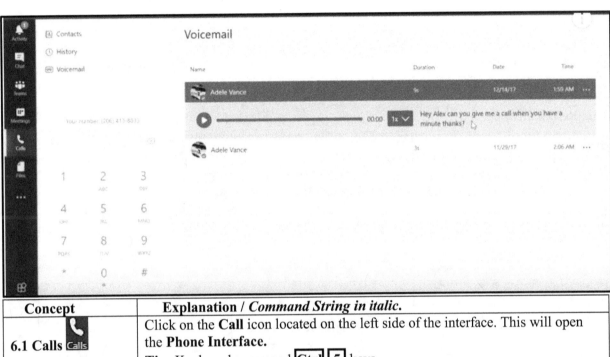

Concept	Explanation / *Command String in italic.*
6.1 Calls Calls	Click on the **Call** icon located on the left side of the interface. This will open the **Phone Interface.** **Tip:** Keyboard command Ctrl 5 keys.
6.2 Calling Plan	You will need a **Calling Plan** to use this phone feature.
6.3 Who Can I Call	Within **Team,** you can call any phone on the planet. (if it is integrated with a **PBX Phone** system).
6.4 Missed Calls	This will allow you to see previous calls or **Missed Calls.**
6.5 Voice Mail	This will allow you to listen to your voicemails.
6.6 Call Queues	This also supports **Call Queues** and calls transferring (if set up).

Chapter 7 - Teamsite (Sites)

A **Teamsite** is a resource pool of information for a department, project team, resource pool, book club, or just general use. **Teamsite** can also centralize common information that is vital to the operation of the company. It can bring the team together from different locations to provide a common working strategy. A **Teamsite** can be created from each project in **Microsoft Teams** which is the resource site for the **Project Team**. A **Teamsite** can also be created in **Sharepoint** as a **Site**, but a **Sharepoint Site** won't be tied or linked to the **Project Team**. A **Teamsite** can contain a **Central Team Calendar**, **Blog**, **Documentation, Text Page** (to explain a process), **Task List,** or whatever you wish to post for the **Team**. You can also build **Subsites** under the **Teamsite** to provide a more focused information bank or for subprojects listed under the **Teams Project Site**. This course will specifically cover the basics of how to develop a **Teamsite** and is not intended to go into the **Sharepoint** development tools.

Chapter Contents:

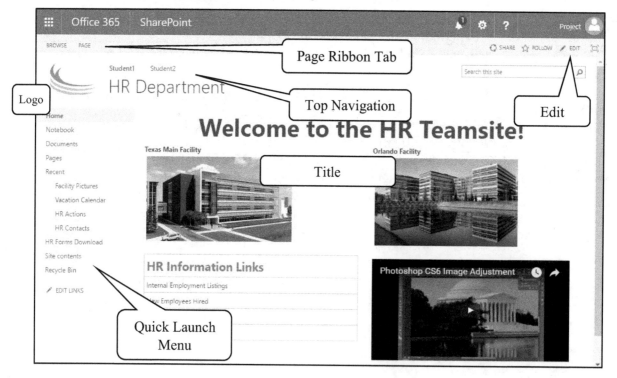

Logo - This is the site logo.

Title - This is the site title.

Quick Launch Area - This is the menu located on the left side of the screen. When additional pages related to this home page are added they will appear here. The **Edit Links** will allow you to change what is listed. The **Home Link** will take you to the home of the active site.

Top Navigation - These are subsites. In the screen to the right, Student1 is a subsite of the main **Teamsite**. For example, you might have a department site and several project sites under the department site.

Page Ribbon Tab - These are additional options to adjust the page layout.

Edit - This will open the **Sharepoint** editing capabilities.

Section 1 - Create A Teamsite

The following will take you through the steps to build a top-level **Teamsite**.

Concept	Explanation / *Command String in italic.*
7.1 Create New Site in Teams	This will build a **Teamsite**. The above is an example of the type of site we will build. This class will create a main training site and students will build subsites under the main **Teamsite**. One way to create a **Teamsite** is to create a **New Team** in **Microsoft Teams**. Then, the **Teamsite** will be automatically created.
Student Project J1 Preparation	This will create a **Teamsite** from **Microsoft Teams**. 1. **Create a new Team in Microsoft Teams:** 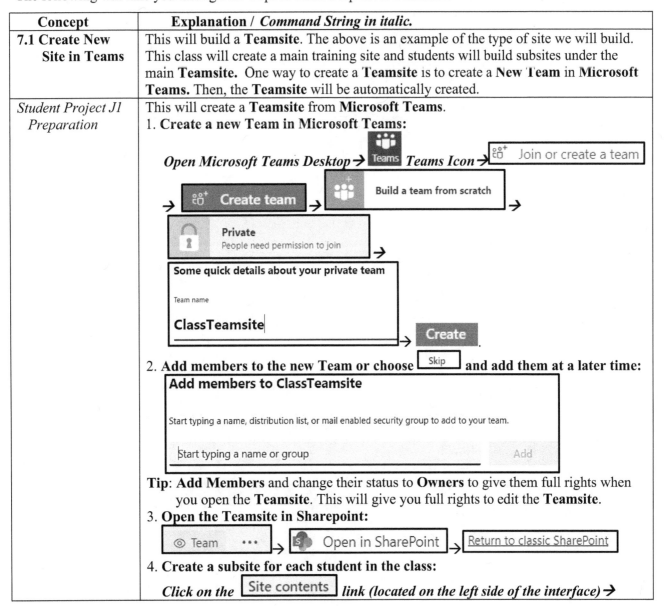 2. **Add members to the new Team or choose** Skip **and add them at a later time:** **Tip: Add Members** and change their status to **Owners** to give them full rights when you open the **Teamsite**. This will give you full rights to edit the **Teamsite**. 3. **Open the Teamsite in Sharepoint:** 4. **Create a subsite for each student in the class:** *Click on the* Site contents *link (located on the left side of the interface)* →

	+ New ⌄		⟋ Site usage	○ Site workflows	⚙ Site settings	🗑 Recycle bin (0)

Contents	Subsites				

	Name	Type	Items	Modified
🗎	Documents	Document library	1	3/13/2020 9:03 PM
🗎	Site Assets	Document library	2	3/13/2020 9:03 PM
🗎	Style Library	Document library	0	3/8/2020 1:54 AM
🗎	Site Pages	Page library	1	3/8/2020 1:54 AM

→ + New ⌄ → Subsite (See next student project).

Section 2 - Create New Subsite

The following will take you through the steps to build a **SubSite**.

Concept	Explanation / *Command String in italic.*
7.2 Create New SubSite	This will build a **Subsite** under the main site or become a **SubTeamsite**. This class will create the main training site and students will build subsites under it.
Student Project J2 Preparation	1. **Create a subsite for each student in the class:** *Click on the* Site contents *link (located on the left side of the interface)* → + New ⌄ Contents Subsites 🔎 Site usage ↻ Site workflows ⚙ Site settings 🗑 Recycle bin (0) Name Type Items Modified Documents Document library 1 3/13/2020 9:03 PM Site Assets Document library 2 3/13/2020 9:03 PM Style Library Document library 0 3/8/2020 1:54 AM Site Pages Page library 1 3/8/2020 1:54 AM → + New ⌄ → Subsite .
Student Project J3 Site Contents	C ✏ EDIT LINKS # Site contents › New SharePoint Site 1. **Title and Description -** This will be the name of the link. Title: Student1 Description: Student1 Teamsite 2. **Web Site Address -** Replace Student1 below with a name for your new site. Record this address to access your new site. URL name: https://ctbinclgon.sharepoint.com/sites/TestTeam/ Student1 3. **Template Selection -** Choose the **Teamsite** option below: Select a language: English Select a template: Collaboration	Enterprise Duet Enterprise Team site (no Office 365 group) Team site (classic experience) Blog Project Site 4. **Permissions -** The parent site will give full permissions to all **Subsites**. User Permissions: ◉ Use same permissions as parent site ◯ Use unique permissions

5. **Navigation -** This will add your site name under the label "**Subsites**" in the **Quick Launch** area.   **Review End**
Result:

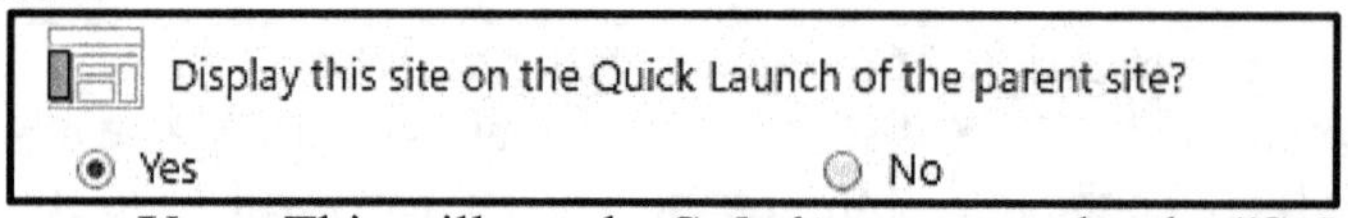

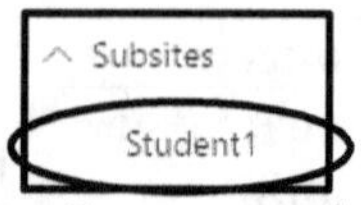

Display this site on the Quick Launch of the parent site?	∧ Subsites
◉ Yes ○ No	Student1

    Yes = This will put the **Subsite** name under the "**Subsites**" menu on the left side of the parent site screen.
    No = The name will not appear on the left side of the screen.

6. **Display on Parent Site -**Your site name will be displayed on the top of the training page.   **Review End Result:**

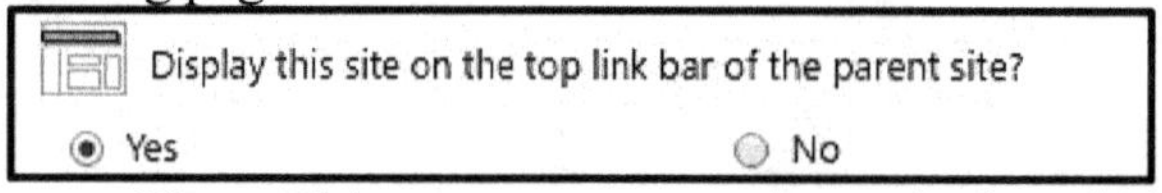

Display this site on the top link bar of the parent site?
◉ Yes   ○ No   Student1   Student2   HR Depart

    Yes = This appears on top above the logo/title on the parent site. It will allow navigation.
    No = The site name will not appear on the top link bar.

7. **Navigation Inheritance -** This will allow your site to inherit the parent's top link bar so you can navigate to other student's subsites.   **Review End Result:**

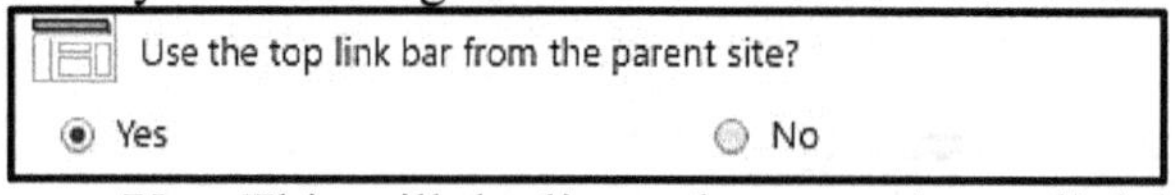

Use the top link bar from the parent site?
◉ Yes   ○ No   Student1   Student2   HR Depart

    Yes=This will duplicate the parent's top link bar to all **Subsites**.
    No=The parent's top bar links will not appear on top of all **Subsites**. Use this if others do not need to navigate between **Subsites**.

8. **The final step to create a SubSite:**

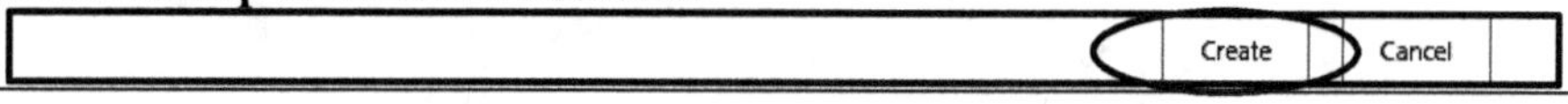

    Create   Cancel

Section 3 - Gear Options

The **Gear Options** are located in the upper right corner of the interface.

Concept	Explanation / *Command String in italic.*
7.3 Gear Options	The **Gear** is located on the top right side of the interface.

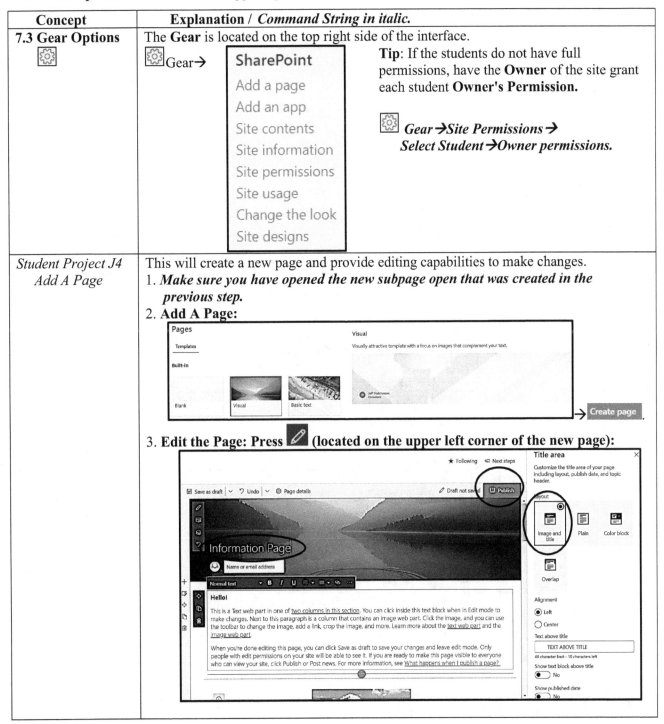

7.3 Gear Options — Gear→ **SharePoint** Add a page / Add an app / Site contents / Site information / Site permissions / Site usage / Change the look / Site designs

Tip: If the students do not have full permissions, have the **Owner** of the site grant each student **Owner's Permission.**

Gear→Site Permissions→ Select Student→Owner permissions.

Student Project J4 Add A Page

This will create a new page and provide editing capabilities to make changes.
1. *Make sure you have opened the new subpage open that was created in the previous step.*
2. **Add A Page:**

3. **Edit the Page: Press** ✏ (located on the upper left corner of the new page):

4. Edit a text box:

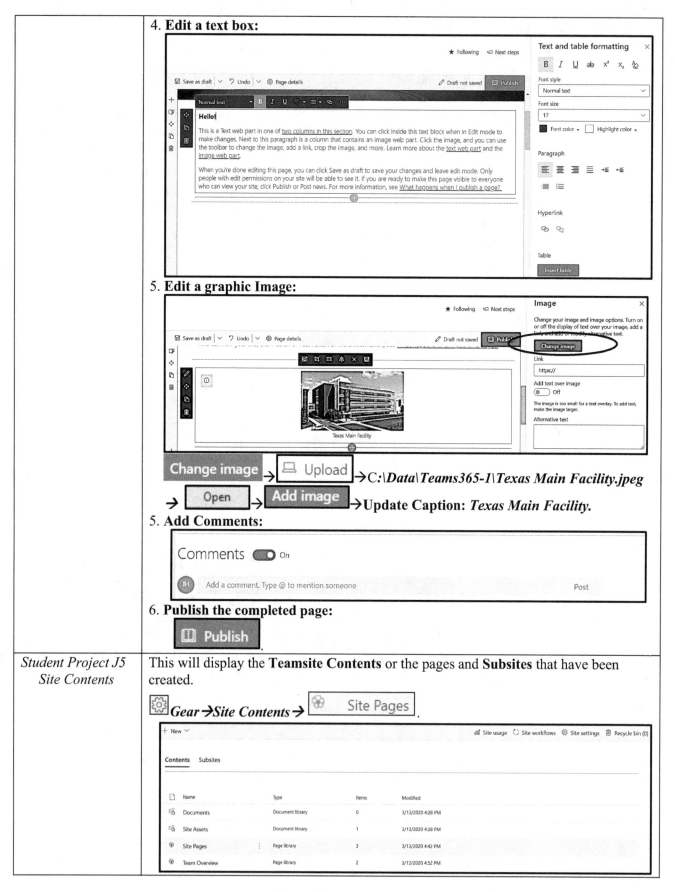

5. Edit a graphic Image:

Change image → Upload → C:\Data\Teams365-1\Texas Main Facility.jpeg

→ Open → Add image → Update Caption: *Texas Main Facility.*

5. Add Comments:

6. Publish the completed page:

Student Project J5 Site Contents	This will display the **Teamsite Contents** or the pages and **Subsites** that have been created. *Gear →Site Contents →* Site Pages

2. This will list the **Site Pages** you have previously created.

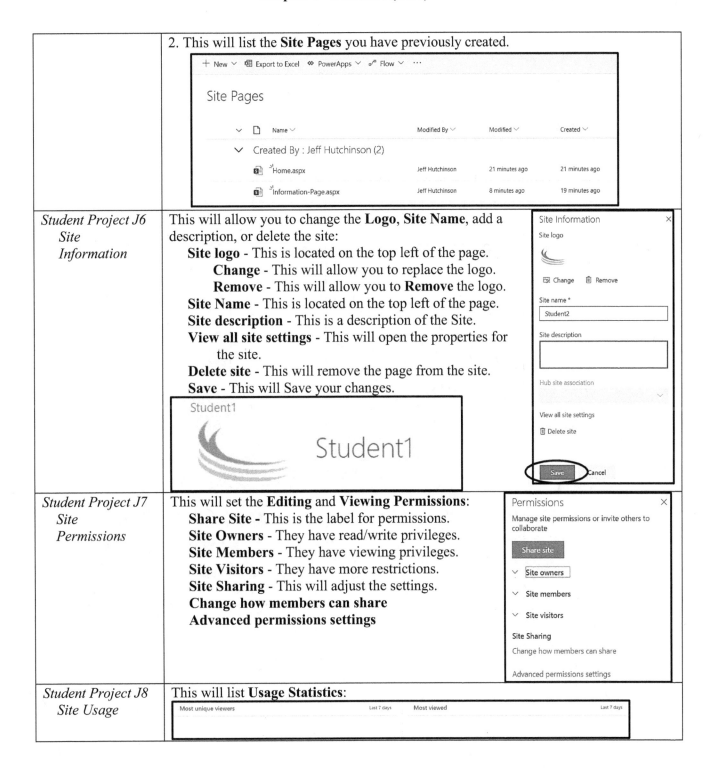

| | Student Project J6 Site Information | This will allow you to change the **Logo, Site Name**, add a description, or delete the site: |

Student Project J6
Site Information

This will allow you to change the **Logo, Site Name**, add a description, or delete the site:

Site logo - This is located on the top left of the page.
    Change - This will allow you to replace the logo.
    Remove - This will allow you to **Remove** the logo.
Site Name - This is located on the top left of the page.
Site description - This is a description of the Site.
View all site settings - This will open the properties for the site.
Delete site - This will remove the page from the site.
Save - This will Save your changes.

Student Project J7
Site Permissions

This will set the **Editing** and **Viewing Permissions**:
Share Site - This is the label for permissions.
Site Owners - They have read/write privileges.
Site Members - They have viewing privileges.
Site Visitors - They have more restrictions.
Site Sharing - This will adjust the settings.
Change how members can share
Advanced permissions settings

Student Project J8
Site Usage

This will list **Usage Statistics**:

Student Project J9 Change The Look	This will change the **Theme** and **Header**. **Save** - This **Saves** the changes. 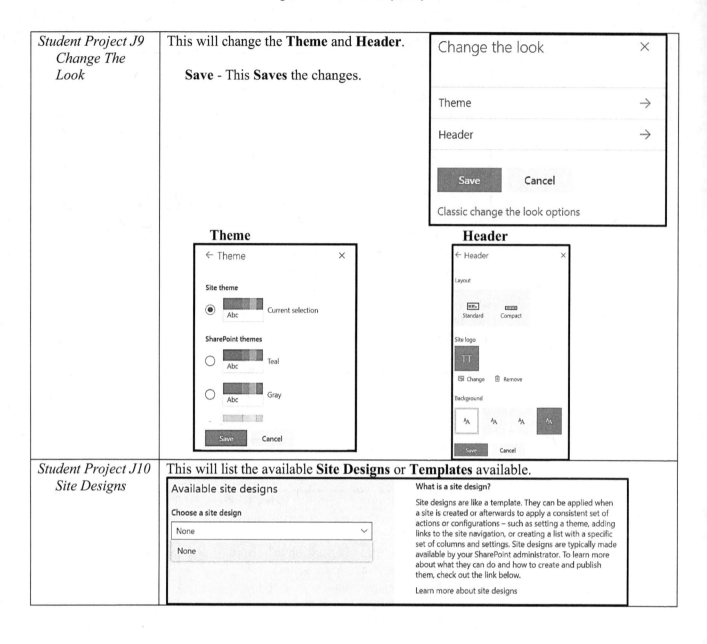
Student Project J10 Site Designs	This will list the available **Site Designs** or **Templates** available.

Section 4 - Add An App

Apps can be added to enhance or provide specific content.

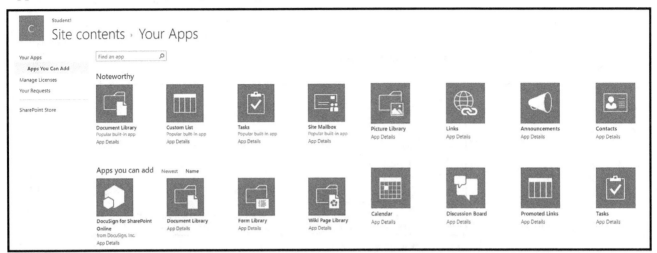

Concept	Explanation / *Command String in italic.*
7.4 Wiki Page Library	A **Wiki Page Library** can be used to provide information or words related to the site.
Student Project J11 Add An App	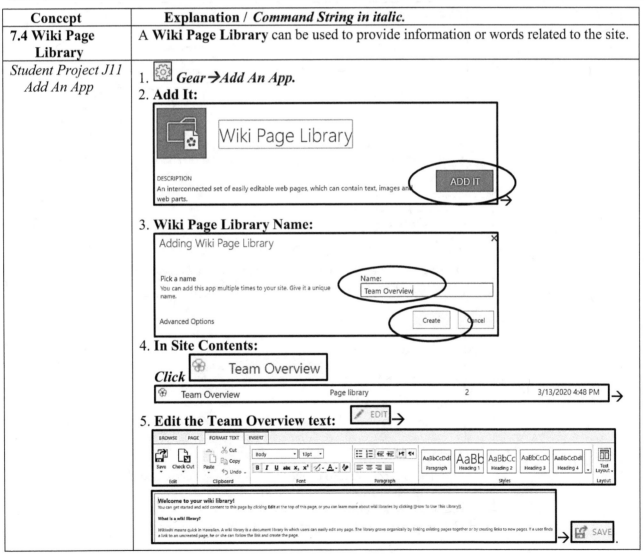

7.5 Document Library	**Libraries** are used to store documentation. Multiple **Libraries** can be created for different purposes. **Document Libraries** are the most popular and allow users to add, edit, check-in/check-out, maintain versioning of documents, and search for a specific document.
Student Project J12 Create New Library	Here, we will create a new **library** and show how to **Upload Files.** 1. ⚙ *Gear→Add An App*. 2. **Add It:** 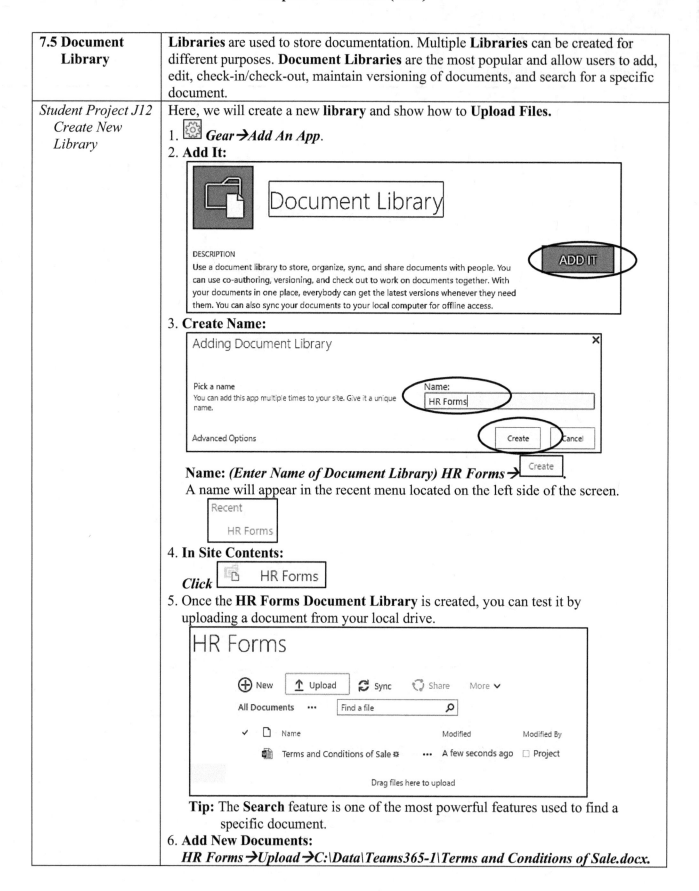 3. **Create Name:** **Name:** *(Enter Name of Document Library) HR Forms →* Create. A name will appear in the recent menu located on the left side of the screen. Recent HR Forms 4. **In Site Contents:** *Click* 🔲 HR Forms 5. Once the **HR Forms Document Library** is created, you can test it by uploading a document from your local drive. **Tip:** The **Search** feature is one of the most powerful features used to find a specific document. 6. **Add New Documents:** *HR Forms→Upload→C:\Data\Teams365-1\Terms and Conditions of Sale.docx.*

Tip: To search for a document, click in the **Search** box located in the upper left corner of the **Document Library** screen:

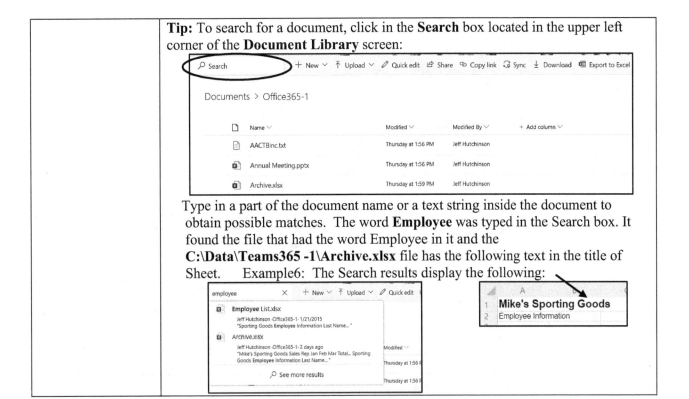

Type in a part of the document name or a text string inside the document to obtain possible matches. The word **Employee** was typed in the Search box. It found the file that had the word Employee in it and the **C:\Data\Teams365 -1\Archive.xlsx** file has the following text in the title of Sheet. Example6: The Search results display the following:

7.6 Contacts List	This can be used to post a common vendor **Contact** information for those who have the right to see this page.

Student Project J13
Add Contacts
	1. ⚙ *Gear→Add An App.*
	2. **Add It:**
	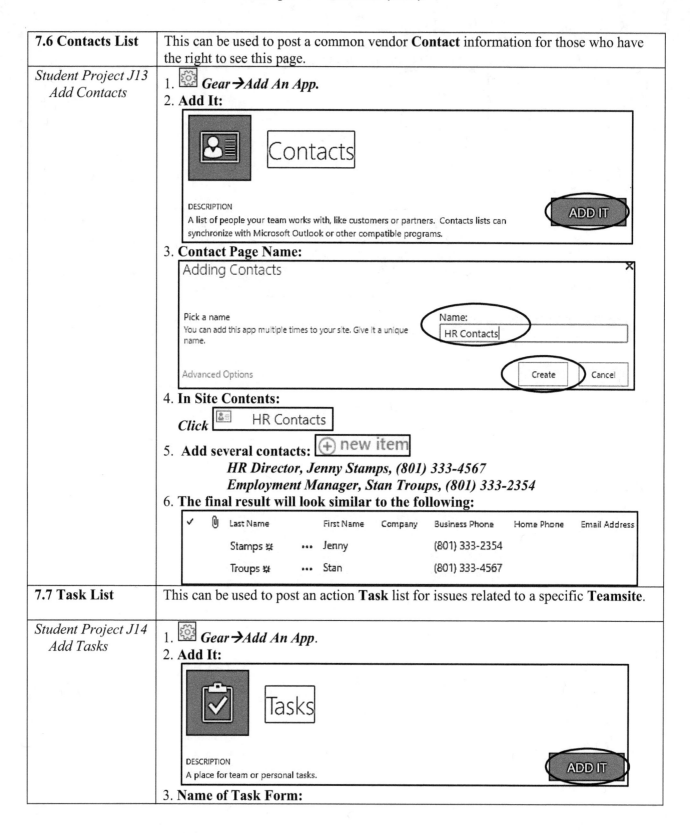
	3. **Contact Page Name:**
	4. **In Site Contents:**
	   Click [HR Contacts]
	5. **Add several contacts:** (+) new item
	      HR Director, Jenny Stamps, (801) 333-4567
	      Employment Manager, Stan Troups, (801) 333-2354
	6. **The final result will look similar to the following:**

✓	📎	Last Name		First Name	Company	Business Phone	Home Phone	Email Address
		Stamps ⌘	•••	Jenny		(801) 333-2354		
		Troups ⌘	•••	Stan		(801) 333-4567		

7.7 Task List	This can be used to post an action **Task** list for issues related to a specific **Teamsite**.
Student Project J14 *Add Tasks*	1. ⚙ *Gear→Add An App.* 2. **Add It:** [Tasks icon] Tasks DESCRIPTION A place for team or personal tasks. ADD IT 3. **Name of Task Form:**

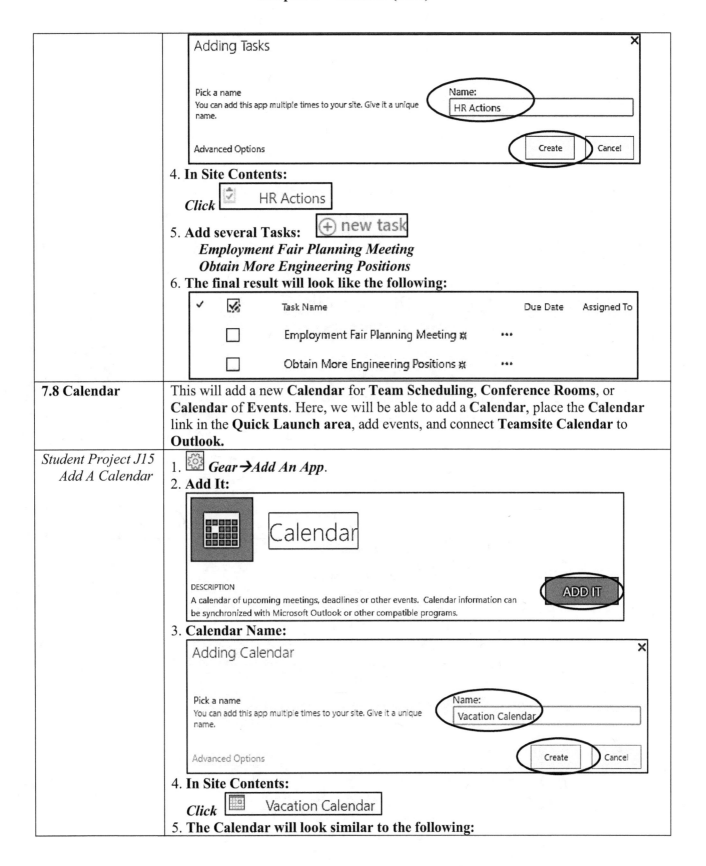

Adding Tasks

Pick a name
You can add this app multiple times to your site. Give it a unique name.

Name:
HR Actions

Advanced Options

Create   Cancel

4. **In Site Contents:**

   Click HR Actions

5. **Add several Tasks:**   ⊕ **new task**
   Employment Fair Planning Meeting
   Obtain More Engineering Positions
6. **The final result will look like the following:**

✓	☑	Task Name		Due Date	Assigned To
	☐	Employment Fair Planning Meeting ✖	•••		
	☐	Obtain More Engineering Positions ✖	•••		

7.8 Calendar	This will add a new **Calendar** for **Team Scheduling**, **Conference Rooms**, or **Calendar** of **Events**. Here, we will be able to add a **Calendar**, place the **Calendar** link in the **Quick Launch area**, add events, and connect **Teamsite Calendar** to **Outlook.**
Student Project J15 Add A Calendar	1. ⚙ *Gear→Add An App.* 2. **Add It:** Calendar DESCRIPTION A calendar of upcoming meetings, deadlines or other events. Calendar information can be synchronized with Microsoft Outlook or other compatible programs. ADD IT 3. **Calendar Name:** Adding Calendar ✕ Pick a name You can add this app multiple times to your site. Give it a unique name. Name: Vacation Calendar Advanced Options Create Cancel 4. **In Site Contents:** *Click* Vacation Calendar 5. **The Calendar will look similar to the following:**

	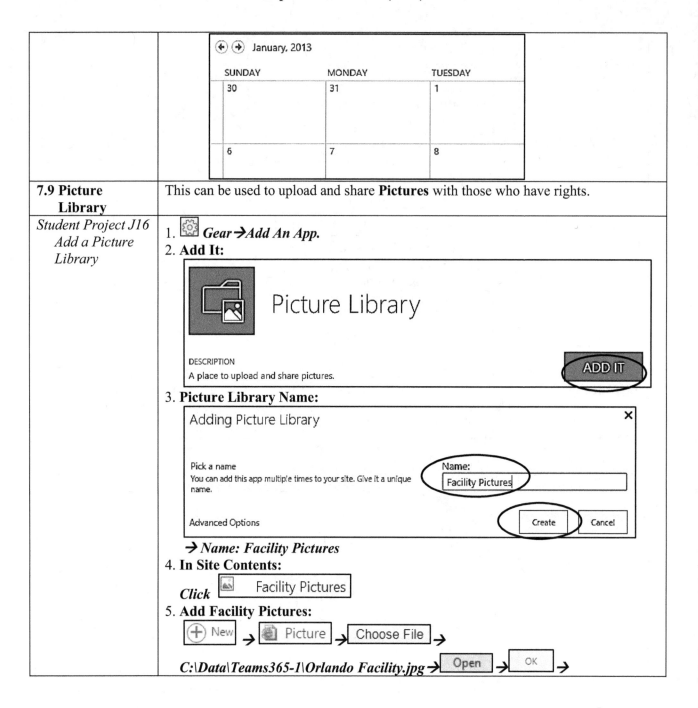
7.9 Picture Library	This can be used to upload and share **Pictures** with those who have rights.
Student Project J16 Add a Picture Library	1. ⚙ *Gear→Add An App.* 2. **Add It:** 3. **Picture Library Name:** → *Name: Facility Pictures* 4. **In Site Contents:** *Click* 🖼 Facility Pictures 5. **Add Facility Pictures:** ⊕ New → 🖼 Picture → Choose File → *C:\Data\Teams365-1\Orlando Facility.jpg* → Open → OK →

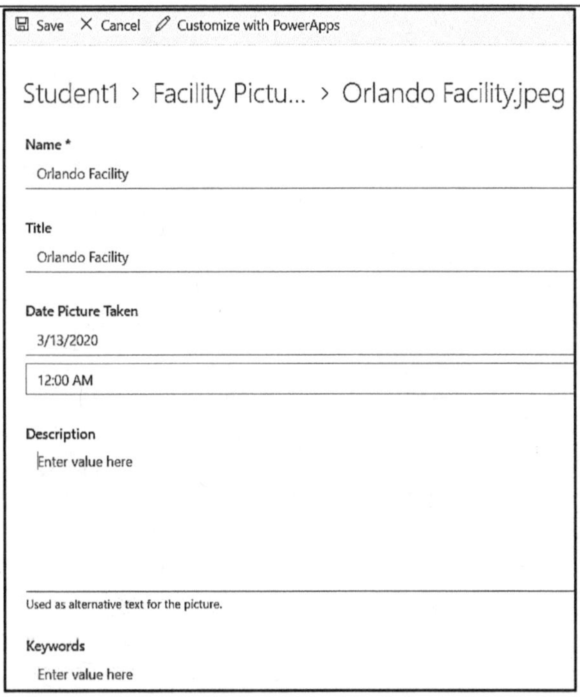

Save ✕ Cancel ✎ Customize with PowerApps

Student1 > Facility Pictu... > Orlando Facility.jpeg

Name *

Orlando Facility

Title

Orlando Facility

Date Picture Taken

3/13/2020

12:00 AM

Description

Enter value here

Used as alternative text for the picture.

Keywords

Enter value here

→ **Save** .

6. Add Facility Pictures:

⊕ New → 🖼 Picture → Choose File →

C:\Data\Teams365-1\Texas Main Facility.jpg → Open → OK →

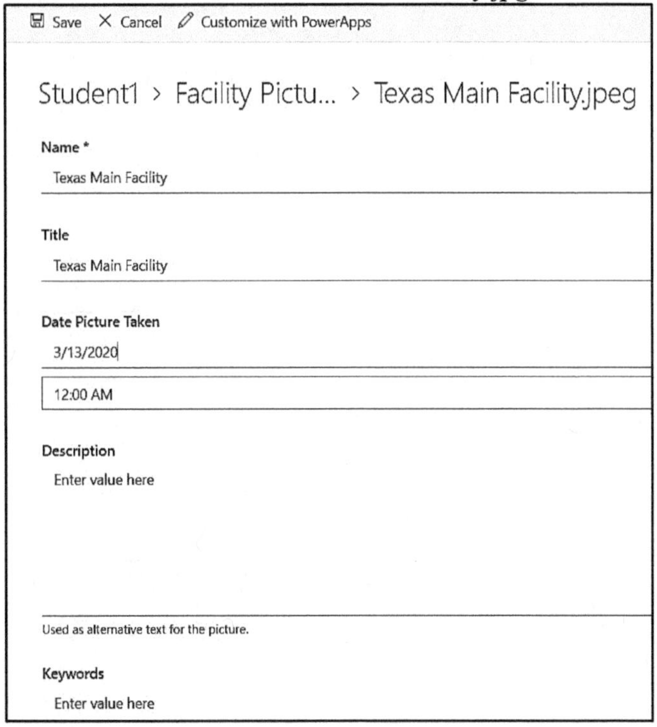

Save ✕ Cancel ✎ Customize with PowerApps

Student1 > Facility Pictu... > Texas Main Facility.jpeg

Name *

Texas Main Facility

Title

Texas Main Facility

Date Picture Taken

3/13/2020

12:00 AM

Description

Enter value here

Used as alternative text for the picture.

Keywords

Enter value here

→ **Save**

7. **The result:**

The following is the final result in Site Contents:

	Name	Type	Items	Modified
	Documents	Document library	0	3/14/2020 1:08 PM
	HR Forms	Document library	1	3/14/2020 1:37 PM
	Site Assets	Document library	5	3/14/2020 1:31 PM
	Facility Pictures	Picture library	2	3/14/2020 2:10 PM
	HR Actions	Tasks list	0	3/14/2020 1:48 PM
	HR Contacts	Contacts list	0	3/14/2020 1:38 PM
	Site Pages	Page library	2	3/14/2020 1:22 PM
	Team Overview	Page library	2	3/14/2020 1:35 PM
	Vacation Calendar	Events list	0	3/14/2020 1:50 PM

Section 5 - Page Ribbon Tab

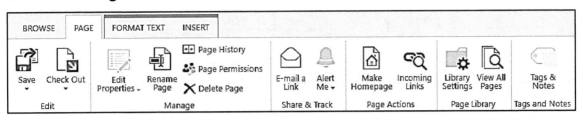

Concept	Explanation / *Command String in italic.*
Student Project K	**In Site Contents→***Click* ⚘ Team Overview → 🖉 EDIT .

Section 6 - Format Text Ribbon Tab

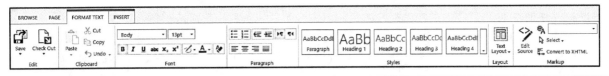

Concept	Explanation / *Command String in italic.*
Student Project L	**In Site Contents→***Click* ⚘ Team Overview → 🖉 EDIT .

Section 7 - Insert Ribbon Tab

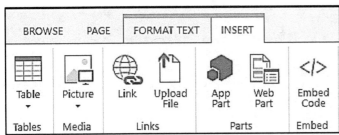

Concept	Explanation / *Command String in italic.*
Student Project M	**In Site Contents→***Click* ⚘ Team Overview → 🖉 EDIT .

Section 8 - Site Settings

Concept	Explanation / *Command String in italic.*
Student Project N	**In Site Contents→***Click* ⚙ Site settings

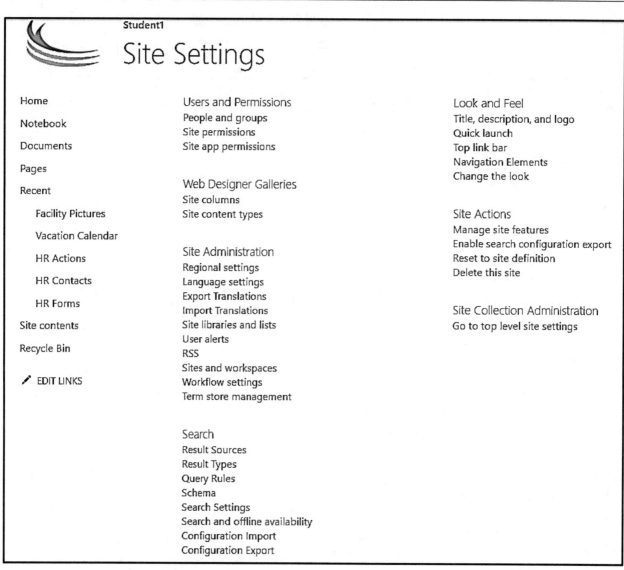

Student1

Site Settings

Home

Notebook

Documents

Pages

Recent

   Facility Pictures

   Vacation Calendar

   HR Actions

   HR Contacts

   HR Forms

Site contents

Recycle Bin

✏ EDIT LINKS

Users and Permissions
People and groups
Site permissions
Site app permissions

Web Designer Galleries
Site columns
Site content types

Site Administration
Regional settings
Language settings
Export Translations
Import Translations
Site libraries and lists
User alerts
RSS
Sites and workspaces
Workflow settings
Term store management

Search
Result Sources
Result Types
Query Rules
Schema
Search Settings
Search and offline availability
Configuration Import
Configuration Export

Look and Feel
Title, description, and logo
Quick launch
Top link bar
Navigation Elements
Change the look

Site Actions
Manage site features
Enable search configuration export
Reset to site definition
Delete this site

Site Collection Administration
Go to top level site settings

Chapter 8 - Apps and Bots

Apps can be added to **Teams** and you will learn there are two different locations where **Apps** can be added. This chapter will focus on the use of **Channel Tabs** and the procedures will indicate placement of the **App**. If you see the word "**Bot**" in the description of the **App** or in the name, then it is an intelligent **App**. **Bots** are short for **Robot** from a software perspective. They provide intelligent automations by responding to you in an intelligent way. You can also carry on a **Chat Conversation** with a **Bot**. One of the most valuable is a **Travel Bot** (such as 🖥 "Ok Roger") that can help find flights and other travel needs.

Chapter Contents

Apps can be added in different locations within **Microsoft Teams.** This chapter will focus on the **Channel** tabs located on the top of the **Channels Chat** area. In the left margin of this workbook, we will indicate if the **App** can be added in **Channels Tabs, Chat Message, Connector App,** or **Personal App.** These different locations will be discussed next:

Channel Tabs

Channels are located on the left side of the interface under a **Team** name. When you select a **Channel**, the **Channel Tab** will appear on the top of the **Channel** interface. You can add many different **Channel Tabs** to provide additional capabilities. The + **Plus** option can be used to customize an interface or add additional **Channel Tabs**. **Tip**: You can **Remove** a **Tab** by selecting the down arrow next to a label and choose **Remove**. If there is no down-arrow the tab, it must be removed by the administrator.

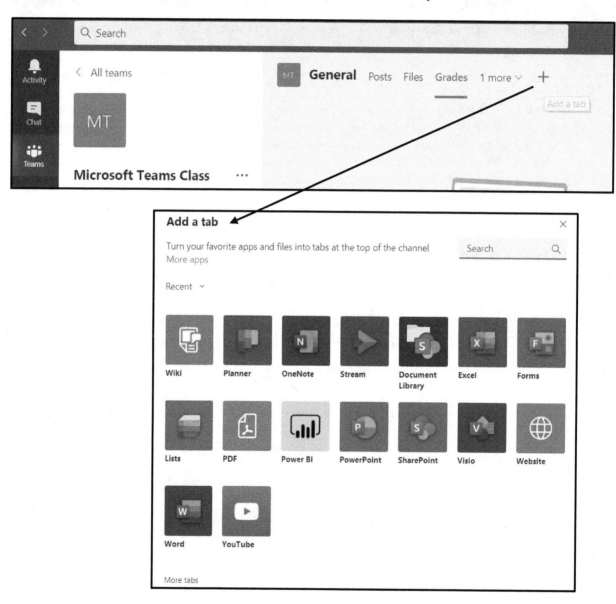

Chat Message App

This type of **App** will allow you to apply **App** directly to a **Chat Message**. This can be done by identifying a **Chat Message**, clicking the ⋯ **More Options**, searching for the **App**, selecting and adding it. Some **Apps** are not available for **Chat Message** which will be indicated in the **Workbook.**

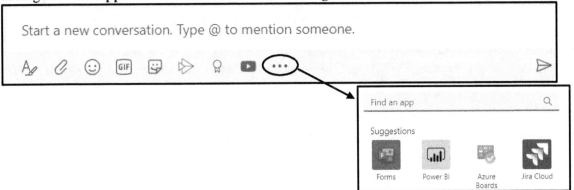

Connectors App

These will allow you to connect a **Channel** to a related **App**. This can be done by identifying a **Channel**, selecting the ⋯ **More Options** to the right of the **Channel** name, and choosing ⌘ Connectors **Connectors**. Some **Apps** are not available for **Connector App** which will be indicated in the **Workbook.** **Tip:** Not available on all systems.

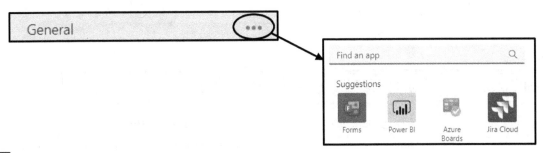

Personal Apps

Personal Apps can be added to the left side of the **Teams** interface and provide the same capability as **Channel Tabs**. When added to the left side of the interface, they are *not* part of the **Channel**, but are available to the logged in user. Some **Apps** are not available for **Channel Tabs** which will be indicated in the **Workbook.**

Section 1 - WiKi Tab

Often, the **Wiki Tab** is added by default. It is used for taking notes or providing information about a **Channel** which is available to everybody on the **Team**. **Wiki** is a **Text Editor** that allows you to make comments and then others can reply to those comments. Each comment is contained in a section and each section supports its **conversation**. **Wiki** content is stored and maintained in **SharePoint**. One interesting feature is able to use **@mention** for inactive **Team Members** or those that don't regularly use the system. **@mention** will notify a person to generate interest. **WiKi** can also be used as an informal **Team** notetaking pad or FAQ's. However, an alternative **App** can be used for taking notes such as **OneNote**,

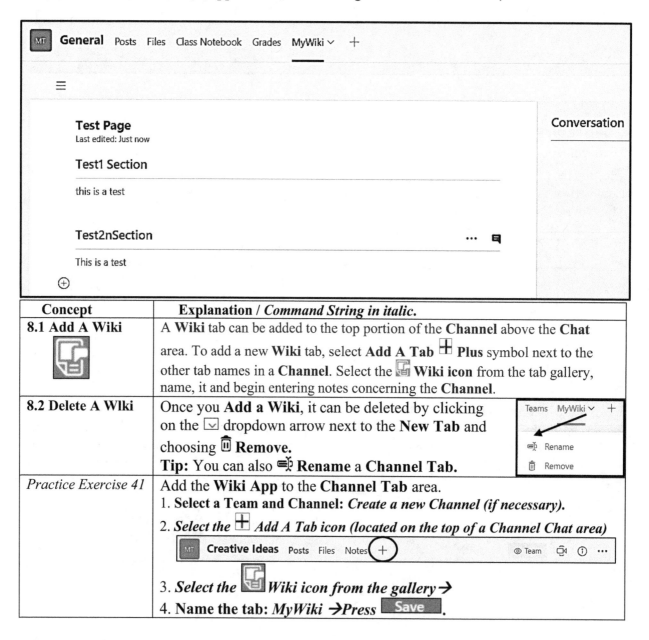

Concept	Explanation / *Command String in italic.*
8.1 Add A Wiki	A **Wiki** tab can be added to the top portion of the **Channel** above the **Chat** area. To add a new **Wiki** tab, select **Add A Tab** ⊞ **Plus** symbol next to the other tab names in a **Channel**. Select the 🔲 **Wiki icon** from the tab gallery, name, it and begin entering notes concerning the **Channel**.
8.2 Delete A Wlki	Once you **Add a Wiki**, it can be deleted by clicking on the ⌄ dropdown arrow next to the **New Tab** and choosing 🗑 **Remove.** Tip: You can also ⇶ **Rename a Channel Tab.**
Practice Exercise 41	Add the **Wiki App** to the **Channel Tab** area. 1. **Select a Team and Channel:** *Create a new Channel (if necessary).* 2. *Select the* ⊞ *Add A Tab icon (located on the top of a Channel Chat area)* 3. *Select the* 🔲 *Wiki icon from the gallery →* 4. **Name the tab:** *MyWiki →Press* `Save` .

	 Tip: Use the above **Wiki** to test the following concepts:
8.3 Format	A **Wiki** tab supports most formatting features such as bold, italic, and underlined text, highlighting, headers, and lists.
8.4 New Page 	The information is stored in a **Page** and every **Page** will have different **Sections**. Multiple **Pages** will appear in the **Navigation Pane**. To create a **New Page**, click on the icon (located on the bottom of the **Wiki** interface). **Pages** can be edited by clicking on the **Navigation Pane**, then choose the ••• **More Options** next to the **Page** name.
8.5 New Section	Multiple **Sections** can be added to each **Page**. To create a **New Section**, click on the Icon. Click on the **Navigation Pane** and choose ••• **More Options** next to the **Page** name. The following options are available:
8.6 Show Section Conversation 	To have a **Conversation** about the comments in the **Section**, click on the **Section** name then click icon (located to the right of the **Section** name). Here, you can post questions, leave comments, or @**mention** your teammates. You have all the same formatting features available in the **Sections**. If someone else has already left comments in the tab conversation, you'll be able to view them in the **Channel** located on the right side of the interface. You'll also know that someone has left comments in your **Wiki** tab because **Show Section Conversation** will appear at the right side of the interface.
8.7 Navigation	Once you create multiple **Pages**, you will see the **Navigation TOC** located on the left side of the screen. This will help you **Navigate** between **Pages** and **Sections**. *Click Navigation to see the Navigation Pane.*
8.8 Copy Link . Red	This will create a hyperlink to the **Page** or **Section**. Click on **Navigation Pane** and choose ••• **More Options** next to the **Page/Section** name, then choose the Copy link.
8.9 Move ↑ **Up**/↓ **Down**	This will change the position of a **Page/Section** in order for the **Wiki Navigation** to be more organized.
8.10 Delete 	This will Delete the **Page** or **Section**. Click on the **Navigation Pane** and choose the ••• **More Options** next to the **Page/Section**, then name choose the Delete.

<table>
<tr>
<td>8.11 @mention</td>
<td>The @mention capability can be used to send an email to someone about comments made in a Section. It can also be used if you want someone to comment or reply to one of your statements. The @mention person will also receive a notification in your Activity feed within Teams.</td>
</tr>
<tr>
<td>Student Project O</td>
<td>Open Microsoft Teams to add Wiki App to the Channel Tab area.
1. Select a Microsoft Teams Class and the General Channel.
2. Select the ⊞ Add A Tab icon (located on the top of a Channel Chat area)

3. Select the Wiki icon from the gallery→
4. Name the tab: Project Overview →Press Save.
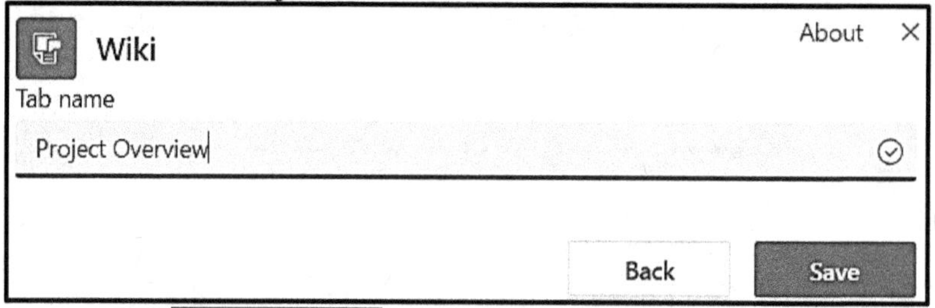

5. Click on the New page icon
(located at the lower left corner of the screen).
6. Click on the Untitled Page text and type in a new name.

7. To create a New Section: Click the Add a new section here Plus sign (locate on the bottom of the Page).
8. Click on the Untitled Page text and type in a new name.

9. Have others in the class provide input by adding random notes such as "How does this work?", or "Can someone reply to this message?", etc.
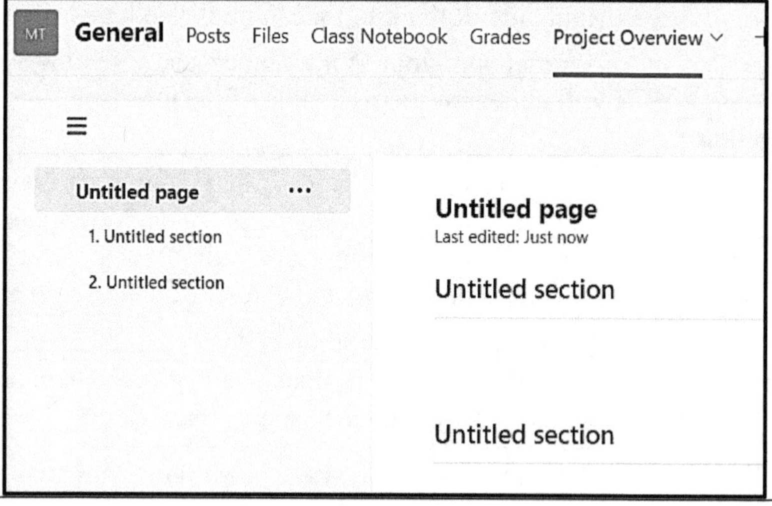
</td>
</tr>
</table>

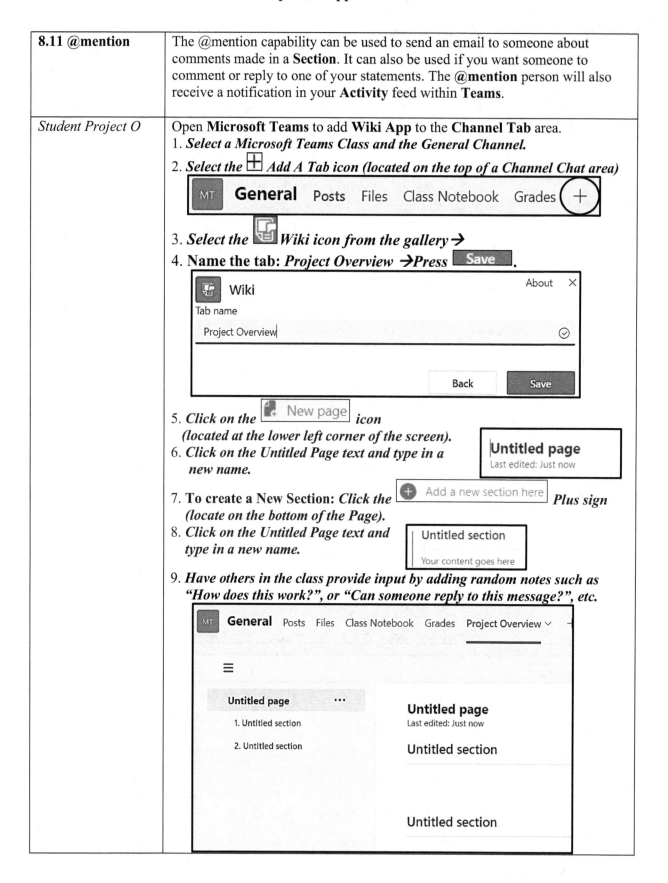

Section 2 - Web site

This can be used to add an **Embedded Link** to a **Web Site** which will appear under the 🌐**Website** tab. This can add additional information related to a **Channel**, or it could be a **Team Web** site or resource related to a **Channel**.

Concept	Explanation / *Command String in italic.*
8.12 Add A Website 🌐	A **Website** tab can be added to the top portion of a **Channel** above the chat area. To add a new **Website**, tab, select **Add A Tab** ⊞ **Plus** symbol next to the other tab names in a **Channel**. Select 🌐 **Website icon** from the tab gallery, name the tab, and enter the URL.
8.13 Delete A Website	Once you **Add a Website**, it can be deleted by clicking on the ⌄ dropdown arrow next to **New Tab** and choosing 🗑 **Remove**. **Tip:** You can also ✒ **Rename** a **Channel Tab** and ⚙ **Settings** will display the original creation screen.
Practice Exercise 42	Add the **Website App** to the **Channel Tab** area. 1. **Select a Team and Channel:** *Create a new Channel (if necessary).* 2. *Select the* ⊞ *Add A Tab icon (located on the top of a Channel Chat area)* 3. *Select the* 🌐*Website icon from the gallery* → **Tab Name:** *Google* URL: *www.google.com* →*Press* **Save** 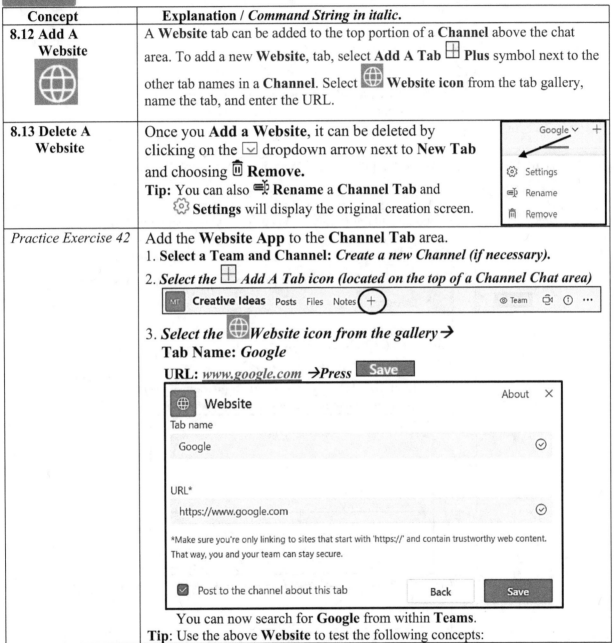 You can now search for **Google** from within **Teams**. **Tip:** Use the above **Website** to test the following concepts:

8.14 Secure Web Site	You need to use a **Secure Website**, so you will have fewer problems. To use a **Secure Website**, use the **HTTPS** prefix such as https://www.test.com (which includes the https prefix). If you use a non-secure site such as http://www.test.com you will get the following message: URL* That isn't a valid URL. http://www.test.com ⓘ
8.15 Display Problems	If your **Website** can't be displayed or refreshed, you will get the following message: If your site isn't loading correctly, ⟨click here⟩ Select the "**Click here**" message and you will receive the following option: ⬀ Go to the site ↻ Reload the tab
8.16 Go To Site ⬀	This will start the **Website** in a separate browser, click the ⬀ icon.
8.17 Reload The Tab ↻	This will **Reload** the opened **Website** in **Microsoft Teams**.
Student Project P Website	Open **Microsoft Teams** to add a **Website App** to the **Channel Tab** area. Have each student add the following **Website** to your assigned **Channel**. Ask others in the class test it out. 1. *Select a Microsoft Teams Class and the General Channel.* 2. *Select the* ⊞ *Add A Tab icon (located on the top of a Channel Chat area)* MT **General** Posts Files Class Notebook Grades Project Overview ⌄ ⊕ 3. *Select the* 🌐 *Website icon from the gallery→* **Enter the Tab Name: elearnlogic** **Enter the URL:** https://www.elearnlogic.com →*Press* **Save** Tip: *Be sure to use a secure site using the prefix of https://* 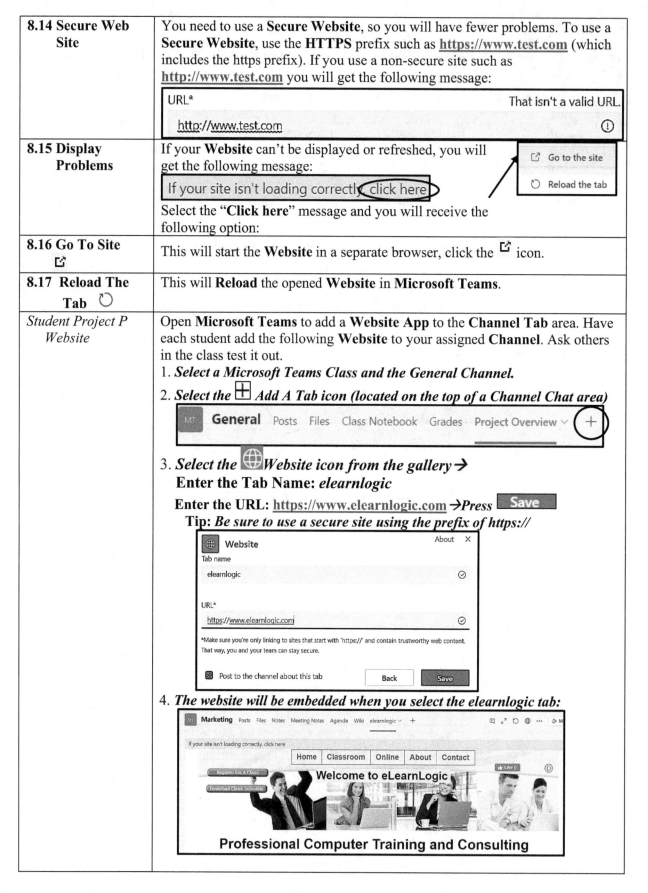 4. *The website will be embedded when you select the elearnlogic tab:*

Section 3 - Power BI Tab

Power BI is a tool used to generate a **Dashboard** of charts describing a data source or other data that is tied to your **Teams Channel**. It provides forecast, status or progress in a chart clarifying information tied to your **Channel**. The following is an example report generated by **Power BI**:

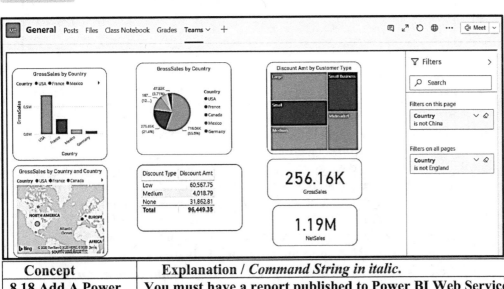

Concept	Explanation / *Command String in italic.*
8.18 Add A Power BI Report	**You must have a report published to Power BI Web Service** in order to display a report. A **Power BI Report** tab can be added to the top portion of a **Channel** above the **Chat Area**. To add a new **Power BI** tab, select **Add A Tab** ⊞ **Plus** symbol next to the other tab names in the **Channel**. Select the ⊞ **Power BI icon** from the tab gallery, name the tab, choose a **Power BI** workspace, then choose the desired report.
8.19 Delete A Power BI Tab	Once you **Add A Power BI Report**, it can be deleted by clicking on the ⌄ dropdown arrow next to the **New Tab** and choosing 🗑 **Remove**. **Tip:** You can also ✎ **Rename** a **Channel Tab** and ⚙ **Settings** will display the original creation screen.
Practice Exercise 43	Add the **Power BI Report App** to the **Channel Tab** area. 1. **Select a Team and Channel:** *Create a new Channel (if necessary).* 2. *Select the* ⊞ *Add A Tab icon (located on the top of a Channel Chat area)* 3. *Select the* ⊞ *Power BI icon from the gallery→* *Name the tab: Teams* *Choose one of the Power BI workspace→ Teams→Press* **Save**

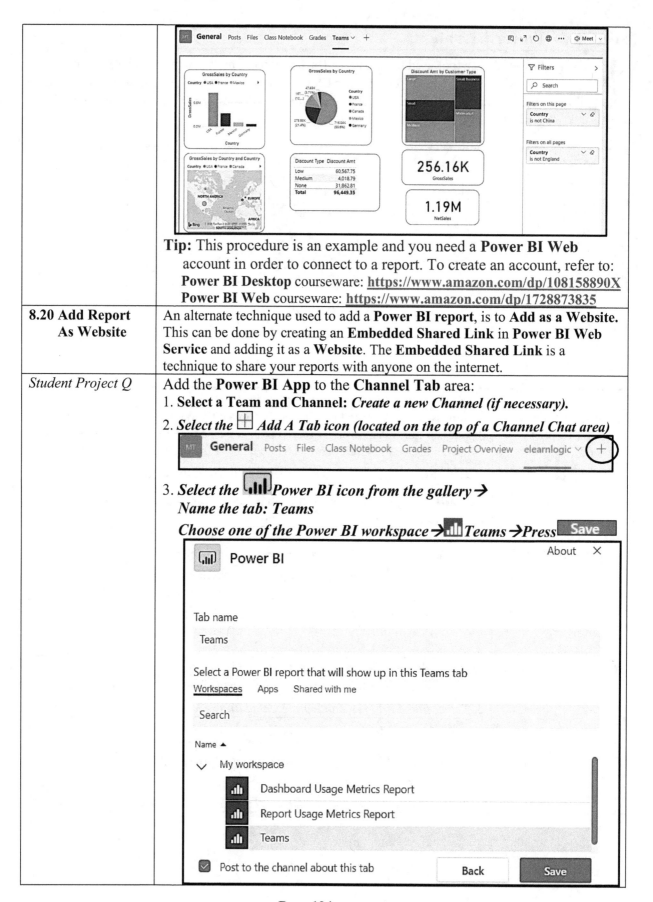

	Tip: This procedure is an example and you need a **Power BI Web** account in order to connect to a report. To create an account, refer to: **Power BI Desktop** courseware: **https://www.amazon.com/dp/108158890X** **Power BI Web** courseware: **https://www.amazon.com/dp/1728873835**
8.20 Add Report As Website	An alternate technique used to add a **Power BI report**, is to **Add as a Website**. This can be done by creating an **Embedded Shared Link** in **Power BI Web Service** and adding it as a **Website**. The **Embedded Shared Link** is a technique to share your reports with anyone on the internet.
Student Project Q	Add the **Power BI App** to the **Channel Tab** area: 1. **Select a Team and Channel:** *Create a new Channel (if necessary).* 2. *Select the* ⊞ *Add A Tab icon (located on the top of a Channel Chat area)* 3. *Select the* Power BI *icon from the gallery* → *Name the tab: Teams* *Choose one of the Power BI workspace* → Teams → Press **Save**

4. *The Power BI report will be displayed as followed:*

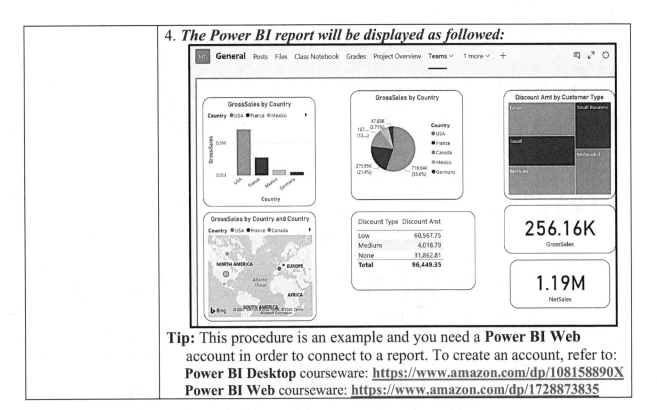

Tip: This procedure is an example and you need a **Power BI Web** account in order to connect to a report. To create an account, refer to:

Power BI Desktop courseware: https://www.amazon.com/dp/108158890X

Power BI Web courseware: https://www.amazon.com/dp/1728873835

Section 4 - OneNote Tab

OneNote is an online **Note Taking** tool. It can be used for taking **Meeting Notes** and can be organized to quickly retrieve notes from specific meetings. There are many other uses for OneNote including research and keeping track of different research categories. If you use **OneNote** on your laptop and are familiar with its capabilities, this can be used as a replacement for the **Wiki App**.

Concept	Explanation / *Command String in italic.*
8.21 Add OneNote	A **OneNote** tab can be added to the top portion of a **Channel** above the chat area. To add a new OneNote tab, select **Add A Tab** ⊞ **Plus** symbol next to the other tab names in the **Channel**. Select the **OneNote icon** from the tab gallery and name the tab.
8.22 Delete the OneNote App	Once you **Add OneNote**, it can be deleted by clicking on the ⌄ dropdown arrow next to the **New Tab** and choosing 🗑 **Remove**. **Tip:** You can also ⇌ **Rename** a **Channel Tab**. MyOneNote ⌄ ⇌ Rename 🗑 Remove
Practice Exercise 44	Add the **OneNote App** to the **Channel Tab** area. 1. **Select a Team and Channel:** *Create a new Channel (if necessary).* 2. *Select the* ⊞ *Add A Tab icon (located on the top of a Channel Chat area)* MT **Creative Ideas** Posts Files Notes (+) 👁 Team ▭ ⓘ ⋯ 3. *Select the OneNote icon from the gallery →* **Tab Name:** *MyOneNote →Press* **Save** 🗒 OneNote About ✕ Use OneNote notebooks to collaborate on digital content and share it with your team. Tab name: MyOneNote ✓ ☑ Post to the channel about this tab Back **Save** **Tip**: Use the above **OneNote** to test the following concepts:
8.23 Navigation >	Once you create multiple pages, you will see the **Navigation Table Of Contents** located on the left side of the screen. This will help you **Navigate** between **Pages**. *Click the* > *to open the Navigation Pane.*

8.24 New Page ☐ + Page	The information is stored in a **Page** and every **Page** can have a **SubPage**. Multiple **Pages** will appear in the **Navigation Pane**. To create a **New Page**, click on the ☐ + Page icon (located on the bottom of the **OneNote** interface). **Pages** can be edited by clicking on the **Navigation Pane** and choose the ••• **More Options** next to the **Page** name. ▸ Copy ▸ Paste ✕ Delete Page ▸ Move/Copy ⊕ New Page → Make Subpage ← Promote Subpage ▸ Show Versions ▸ Copy Link to this Page ↗ Open in new tab
8.25 SubPage	When you insert 2 pages, you can **Right-click** on page 2 and make it a **SubPage**. **Right-click on Page2**→ → Make Subpage **Tip:** The first page in a **Navigation Pane** cannot be a **SubPage**.
8.26 Sections	This **App** does not support sections, but the **Microsoft OneNote** application does. **Install** or **Open** the **OneNote Application** on your desktop to review the **Sections** tied to each page located on the right-side of the interface.
8.27 Copy/Paste	This will allow you to use the standard ▸Copy and ▸Paste feature to duplicate a Page. *Click on the Navigation Pane→Right-click on a Page name→Choose ▸ Copy and then, ▸Paste.*
8.28 Delete ✕	This will allow you to ✕ **Delete** a selected **Page**. *Click on the Navigation Pane →Right-click any Page →Press ✕Delete.*
8.29 Move/Copy	This will allow you to ▸Move or ▸Copy a **Page** to another **OneNote** tab or any **OneNote** item that appears in the list. *Click on the Navigation Pane→Right-click on a Page name→Choose ▸Move or ▸Copy.*
8.30 Make SubPage →	This will allow you to create a → **SubPage**. *Click on the Navigation Pane →Right-click on any page other than the Top Page→ → Make SubPage.*
8.31 Promote SubPage ←	This will allow you to turn a **SubPage** into a main page. *Click on the Navigation Pane →Right-click on a SubPage Name → Choose ←Promote SubPage.*
8.32 Show/Hide Versions	This will display **Who** created the **Page** and the **Date** it was created. Untitled Page 9/6/2020 Jeff Hutchinson
8.33 Copy Link To This Page	This will create a hyperlink to the selected **Page**. This hyperlink can be emailed to interested people for quick access to the **OneNote App**. *Click on the Navigation Pane →Right-click on the Page→ Choose ▸ Copy Link To This Page.*
8.34 Open In New Tab ↗	This will open the **OneNote Tab** in a web browser. *Click on the Navigation Pane →Right-click on the Page→ Choose ↗ Open On New Tab.*
8.35 Home Ribbon Tab	The **Home Ribbon Tab** provides the standard formatting capability needed. File Home Insert Draw View Help Open in browser ∨ ? Tell me what you want to do ↺∨ ☐∨ Calibri Light ∨ 20 ∨ B I U ✏∨ A∨ ✂ A̲ ••• ☰∨ ☰∨ ••• A∨ ✎∨ ✎∨ ☐∨

8.36 Insert Ribbon Tab	The **Insert Ribbon Tab** will allow you to insert pictures, files, links, etc. 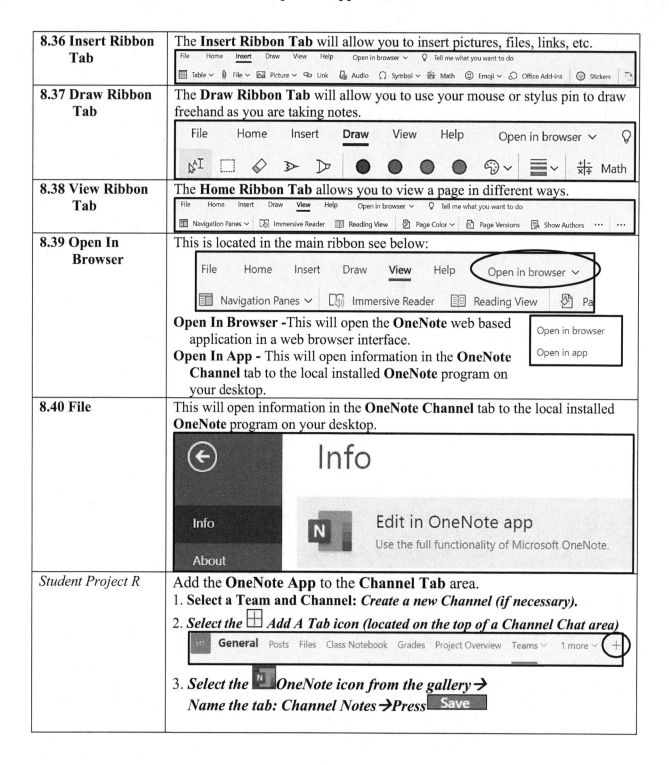
8.37 Draw Ribbon Tab	The **Draw Ribbon Tab** will allow you to use your mouse or stylus pin to draw freehand as you are taking notes.
8.38 View Ribbon Tab	The **Home Ribbon Tab** allows you to view a page in different ways.
8.39 Open In Browser	This is located in the main ribbon see below: **Open In Browser -**This will open the **OneNote** web based application in a web browser interface. **Open In App -** This will open information in the **OneNote Channel** tab to the local installed **OneNote** program on your desktop.
8.40 File	This will open information in the **OneNote Channel** tab to the local installed **OneNote** program on your desktop.
Student Project R	Add the **OneNote App** to the **Channel Tab** area. 1. **Select a Team and Channel:** *Create a new Channel (if necessary).* 2. *Select the* ⊞ *Add A Tab icon (located on the top of a Channel Chat area)* 3. *Select the* OneNote *icon from the gallery* → *Name the tab: Channel Notes* → *Press* Save

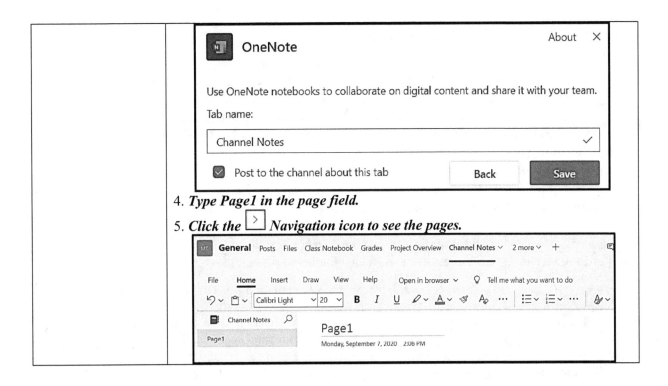

4. *Type Page1 in the page field.*

5. *Click the ⟩ Navigation icon to see the pages.*

Section 5 - Stream Tab (Video App)

 This is **Sharepoint Video Library** or video service available to **Microsoft Teams**. It is used to store/view **Recorded Videos** for **Teams Meetings** or upload any recorded video. When you start a **Meeting** from a **Channel** and choose to record it, a link is placed in a **Chat Message**. The recorded meeting is actually stored in the **Stream** storage location. If you **Record** a **Meeting** and can't find the **Recording** after the **Meeting**, you can search **Stream** to find it. You can search the name of the meeting or date range when the meeting took place. If you have ongoing meeting or events, be sure to name the **Meeting** with a naming sequence such as Lunch-N-Learn March 2021, Lunch-N-Learn April 2021, Lunch-N-Learn May 2021, etc. Also, make sure your meeting name is descriptive enough so others can also find the related **Recorded Meeting**.

Concept	Explanation / *Command String in italic.*
8.41 Add A Stream Video	A **Stream** tab can be added to the top portion of a **Channel** above the chat area. To add a new Stream tab, select the **Add A Tab** ⊞ **Plus** symbol next to the other tab names in the **Channel**. Select the Stream icon from the tab gallery, name the tab, search the **Video**, and select the **URL**.
8.42 Delete A Stream App	Once you **Add A Stream Tab**, it can be deleted by clicking on the ⌄ dropdown arrow next to the **New Tab** and choosing 🗑 **Remove.** **Tip:** You can also ✎ **Rename** a **Channel Tab** and the ⚙ **Settings** will display the original creation screen.
Practice Exercise 45	Add the **Stream App** to the **Channel Tab** area. 1. **Select a Team and Channel:** *Create a new Channel (if necessary).* 2. *Select the* ⊞ *Add A Tab icon (located on the top of a Channel Chat area)* 3. *Select the Stream icon from the gallery* → ⦿ **Video** **Search or paste: Leadership** *(Type Video, test, meeting, etc. until you find video to add).* **Tab Name: Leadership** → *Press* **Save**.

In the 8.42 cell image:
Leadership ⌄
⚙ Settings
✎ Rename
🗑 Remove

In Practice Exercise 45 cell images:
MT **Creative Ideas** Posts Files Notes (+) 👁 Team 📷 ⓘ ···

Stream   About ✕
○ Channel ⦿ Video
Search or paste a direct link to a Microsoft Stream video
What is Leadership? ✕
Tab name
Leadership
☑ Post to the channel about this tab   Back   Save

Student Project S	Whenever a **Video** is recorded in **Teams,** it is automatically stored in **Microsoft Streams.** This will add the **Stream App** to the **Channel Tab** area. 1. **Select a Team and Channel:** *Create a new Channel (if necessary).* 2. *Select the* ⊞ *Add A Tab icon (located on the top of a Channel Chat area)* 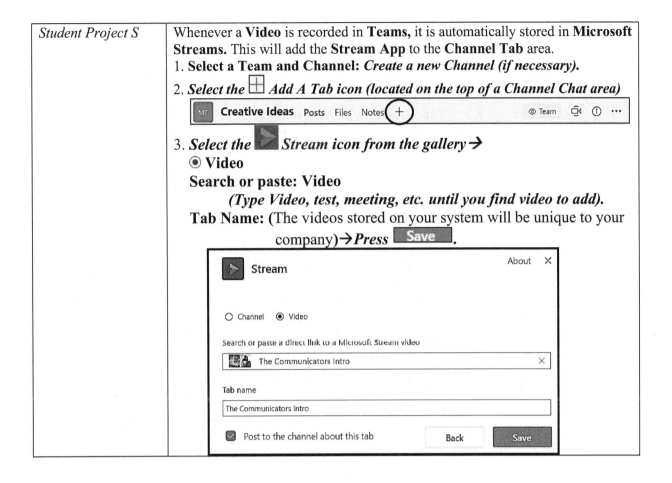

Section 6 - YouTube App

 This will allow you to link to a **YouTube** video at **Youtube.com**. This can be helpful if you have a training **YouTube Video** that you want a **Team** to review. Storing this material in **Teams** provides a quick reference as opposed to having to go out of your way to search for **Videos** on **YouTube**. This will keep a **Team** focused by providing easily accessible and shared videos available to members in the **Channel**.

Concept	Explanation / *Command String in italic.*
8.43 Add YouTube	A **YouTube** tab can be added to the top portion of a **Channel** above the chat area. To add a new YouTube tab, select **Add A Tab** next to the other tab names in the **Channel**. Select the YouTube icon from the tab gallery, name the tab, **Search** for a **Video** on **YouTube**, and Select the desired **Video**.
8.44 Delete A YouTube App	Once you **Add A YouTube Video,** it can be deleted by clicking on the ⌄ dropdown arrow next to the **New Tab** and choosing 🗑 **Remove.** **Tip:** You can also ✍ **Rename** a **Channel Tab.**
Practice Exercise 46	Add the **YouTube App** to the **Channel Tab** area: 1. **Select a Team and Channel:** *Create a new Channel (if necessary).* 2. *Select the* ⊞ *Add A Tab icon (located on the top of a Channel Chat area)* 3. *Select the* YouTube *icon from the gallery* → **Search For: Power BI Jeff Hutchinson** → Select the desired Video → *Press* Save *.*
Student Project T	Add the **YouTube App** to the **Channel Tab** area. 1. **Select a Team and Channel:** *Create a new Channel (if necessary).* 2. *Select the* ⊞ *Add A Tab icon (located on the top of a Channel Chat area)* 3. *Select the* YouTube *icon from the gallery* → **Search For: Power BI Jeff Hutchinson** → Select the desired Video → *Press* Save *.*

4. *The Channel will now have a Youtube App similar to the following:*

Section 7 - Planner

Planner will allow your team to be more organized by assigning **Tasks** and keeping track of your progress on a daily basis. You can create a **New Plan** or use an **Existing Plan** stored in another **Channel**. This will allow you to cross over several **Channels** that relate to your **Team**. **Planner** will allow you to set objectives and then **Assign Tasks** to a specific objective.

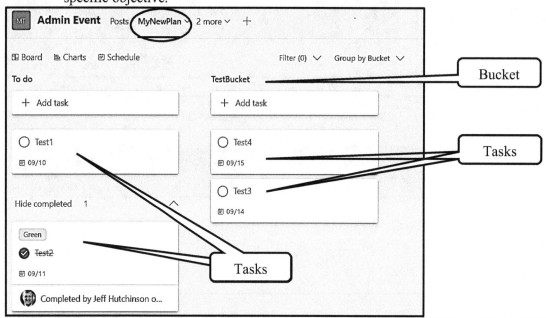

Concept	Explanation / *Command String in italic.*
8.45 Add Planner	A **Planner** tab can be added to the top portion of a **Channel** above the chat area. To add a new Planner tab, select **Add A Tab** ⊞ **Plus** symbol next to the other tab names in the **Channel**. Select the Planner icon from the tab gallery, check **Create a New Plan**, and enter a **Plan Name**.
8.46 Delete A Planner App	Once you **Add A Planner App,** it can be deleted by clicking on the ☑ dropdown arrow next to the **New Tab** and choosing 🗑 **Remove.** **Tip:** You can also ✎ **Rename** a **Channel Tab** and the ⚙ **Settings** will display the original creation screen.
Practice Exercise 47	Add the **Planner App** to the **Channel Tab** area. 1. **Select a Team and Channel:** *Create a new Channel (if necessary).* 2. *Select the* ⊞ *Add A Tab icon (located on the top of a Channel Chat area)* 3. *Select the Planner icon from the gallery→ Press* **Add** 4. *Press* ⊙ *Create a new plan→Enter the Tab Name: MyNewPlan→*

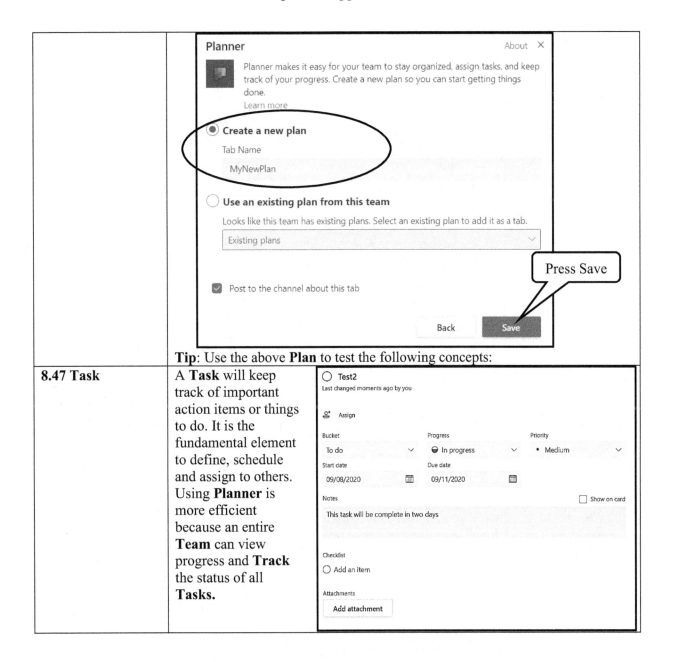

Tip: Use the above **Plan** to test the following concepts:

8.47 Task	A **Task** will keep track of important action items or things to do. It is the fundamental element to define, schedule and assign to others. Using **Planner** is more efficient because an entire **Team** can view progress and **Track** the status of all **Tasks.**	

8.48 Task Options	Each **Task** will have a set of options. ***Click on the [...] More Options button to see available options.*** [Label icon] **Label** - This will color code a **Task** with the following colors: Pink, Red, Yellow, Green, Blue, and Purple. [Assign icon] **Assign** - This will **Assign** a **Task** to another person. [Copy icon] **Copy Task** - This will copy a **Task** to a different **Plan** or **Bucket**. [Copy Link icon] **Copy Link To Task** - This will create a hyperlink to a **Task**. Press the Ctrl C keys to copy the **Link** and Ctrl V keys to Paste it in your email. [Move icon] **Move Task** - This will change the position of a **Task** for better organization. [Delete icon] **Delete** - This will [trash icon] **Delete** a **Task**.
8.49 Board [board icon]	**Tasks** and **Buckets** will be stored in the **Board** area. ***Click on the [board icon] Board button to see a list of Tasks that have been added.***
8.50 Add New Bucket Add new bucket	**Buckets** will contain groups of **Tasks**. Each group of buckets will be a different subject or objective you are trying to accomplish. ***Click on option "Add New Bucket" to start a new group.***
8.51 Completed Task [check icon]	Click the [check icon] **Checkbox** in front of a **Task** to indicate it is complete.
8.52 Chart [chart icon]	Once you create **Tasks**, you can produce a **Chart** to display statistics as needed. It will show the number of tasks in progress, late tasks, and completed **Tasks**.
8.53 Schedule [schedule icon]	This will display a **Calendar** of [icon] **Scheduled Tasks**.

8.54 Filter	When you have many active **Tasks** and **Buckets** defined, you can **Filter** them to find what is needed. **Filter** - Type in the keyword of the **Task**. **Due** - This displays **Tasks** by **Due Date**. **Late** - This displays **Tasks** if **Late**. **Today** - This displays **Tasks** if due **Today**. **Tomorrow** - This displays **Tasks** due **Tomorrow**. **This Week** - This displays **Tasks** due **This Week**. **Next Week** - This displays **Tasks** due **Next Week**. **Future** - This displays **Tasks** due in the **Future**. **No Date** - This displays **Tasks** that have no **Due Date**.
8.55 Group By	You can display **Tasks** based on a **Grouping** of **Buckets**, **Assigned To, Progress, Due Date, Labels** and **Priority**.
Student Project U	Add the **Planner App** to the **Channel Tab** area. 1. *Open Microsoft Teams→ Press* ⊞ *(located on the top of a Channel)→ Choose the* ▧ *Planner App Icon→ Press* **Add** *(To add the* ▧ *Planner App).* 2. *Press* ◉ *Create a new plan→Enter the Tab Name: MyNewTeam→* 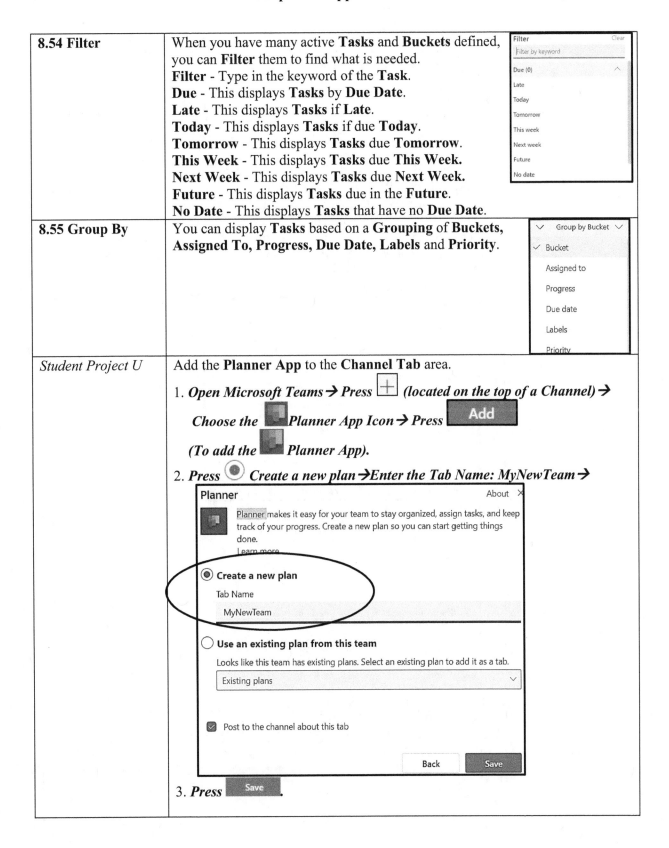 3. *Press* **Save** .

4. *The Channel will now have a Planner App similar to the following:*

5. **Add New Bucket called:** *Build Team and add the following Tasks:*
   Create Team (Schedule Tomorrow)
   Identify Members (Schedule in 2-days)
   Schedule Meeting (Schedule in 3-days).
6. *Add New Bucket called: Create Channels and add the following Tasks:*
   Identify Channels (Schedule in 2-days)
   Document Purpose (Schedule in 3-days)
7. *Tasks will look similar to the following:*

8. *Open "Create Team" Task and make the following changes:*

9. **Filter by:** *Today*

10. **Group it by:** *Group by Bucket.*

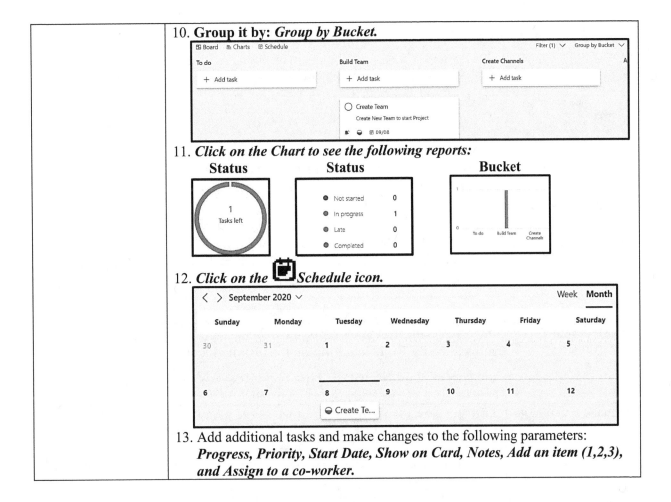

11. *Click on the Chart to see the following reports:*

12. *Click on the* Schedule *icon.*

13. Add additional tasks and make changes to the following parameters: *Progress, Priority, Start Date, Show on Card, Notes, Add an item (1,2,3), and Assign to a co-worker.*

Section 8 - News App

This will allow you to stay on top of the latest news and current events. **News** is pulled from the **Bing News** website which is on top of the latest news developments. This **App** can be added as a **Chat Message App** or a **Personal App**.

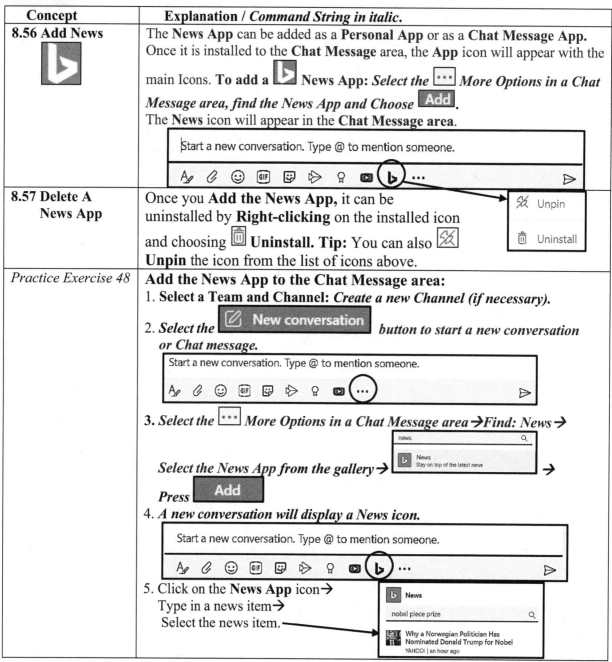

Concept	Explanation / *Command String in italic.*
8.56 Add News	The **News App** can be added as a **Personal App** or as a **Chat Message App**. Once it is installed to the **Chat Message** area, the **App** icon will appear with the main Icons. **To add a** News App: *Select the* ⋯ *More Options in a Chat Message area, find the News App and Choose* **Add**. The **News** icon will appear in the **Chat Message** area.
8.57 Delete A News App	Once you **Add the News App**, it can be uninstalled by **Right-clicking** on the installed icon and choosing 🗑 **Uninstall. Tip:** You can also ✂ **Unpin** the icon from the list of icons above.
Practice Exercise 48	Add the News App to the Chat Message area: 1. **Select a Team and Channel:** *Create a new Channel (if necessary).* 2. *Select the* **New conversation** *button to start a new conversation or Chat message.* 3. *Select the* ⋯ *More Options in a Chat Message area→Find: News→ Select the News App from the gallery→ Press* **Add** 4. *A new conversation will display a News icon.* 5. Click on the **News App** icon→ Type in a news item→ Select the news item.

Section 9 - Weather App

This will find active weather reports when you type in your City, Zip Code, or any location.

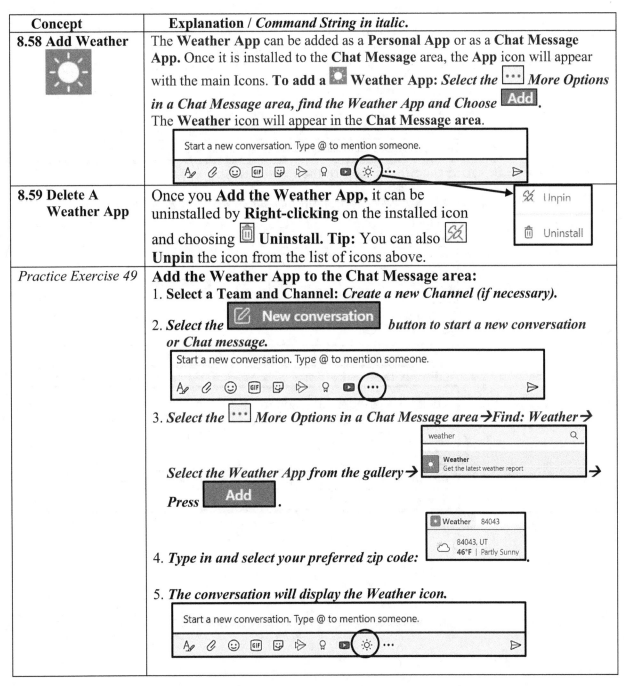

Concept	Explanation / *Command String in italic.*
8.58 Add Weather	The **Weather App** can be added as a **Personal App** or as a **Chat Message App.** Once it is installed to the **Chat Message** area, the **App** icon will appear with the main Icons. **To add a** ☀ **Weather App:** *Select the* ⋯ *More Options in a Chat Message area, find the Weather App and Choose* **Add** . The **Weather** icon will appear in the **Chat Message area.**
8.59 Delete A Weather App	Once you **Add the Weather App,** it can be uninstalled by **Right-clicking** on the installed icon and choosing 🗑 **Uninstall. Tip:** You can also ✂ **Unpin** the icon from the list of icons above.
Practice Exercise 49	**Add the Weather App to the Chat Message area:** 1. **Select a Team and Channel:** *Create a new Channel (if necessary).* 2. *Select the* **New conversation** *button to start a new conversation or Chat message.* 3. *Select the* ⋯ *More Options in a Chat Message area→Find: Weather→ Select the Weather App from the gallery→ Press* **Add** . 4. *Type in and select your preferred zip code:* 5. *The conversation will display the Weather icon.*

Section 10 - Stock App

This will display the current **Stock** rate based on a **Stock Symbol** entered.

Concept	Explanation / *Command String in italic.*
8.60 Add Stock App	The Stock App can be added as a **Personal App** or as a **Chat Message App.** Once it is installed to a **Personal** area, the **App** icon will not appear with the main Icons, but will be available in the search box located on the top of the interface. **To add a Stock App:** *Select the* More Options in a Personal App area, find the Stock App and Choose Add. The **Stock** icon will appear in the search box located on top of the interface. Stocks [Enter a stock symbol] ×
Practice Exercise 50	**Add the Stocks App to the Personal App area:** 1. *Select* More Options located on the left side of the Teams interface. 2. **Find:** *Stock → Select the Stock App from the gallery →* Stocks Stocks Get real-time stock quotes → *Press* Add 3. *The Stock icon will appear in the search box located on top of the interface.* Stocks [Enter a stock symbol] × 4. **To display the Stock App:** *Type @Stock in the search area.* Look for messages, files, and more. Or type / for a list of commands. @Stocks 5. *Select @Stock and the following will be displayed:* Stocks [Enter a stock symbol] ×

Index - Microsoft Teams

Microsoft Office Courseware
Step-By-Step Training Guide and Workbook
Available on Amazon.com (Search for author, Jeff Hutchinson)

These **Step-By-Step Training Guides** focus on specific learning concepts including brief descriptions as well as many short 2-5 minute exercises for practice. The Table of Contents and Index will allow students to look up desired concepts quickly and easily. These guides are invaluable resources to build and maintain computer skills for industry, as well as for personal use.

Available in Paperback: $9.95 or Kindle eBook: $5.95

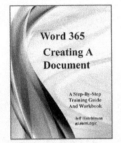
https://www.amazon.com /dp/B085P3R77X

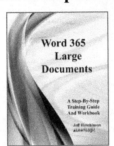
https://www.amazon.com /dp/B084D2WDLG

https://www.amazon.com /dp/B0882ZM5Z7

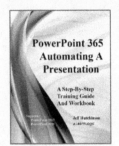
https://www.amazon.com /dp/B08833D3YX

https://www.amazon.com /dp/B084CZGG4B

https://www.amazon.com /dp/B084DHKMY8

https://www.amazon.com /dp/B084D7V4DD

https://www.amazon.com /dp/B078QTH5JZ

About the Author

Jeff Hutchinson is a corporate computer trainer and consultant who teaches **Microsoft** and **Adobe** products from beginning to advanced topics. He has a BS degree from BYU in Computer-Aided Engineering and owned a computer training and consulting firm in San Francisco, California for several years. He currently works as an independent computer instructor using his training guides and courseware to teach students remote online all over the world.

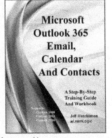
https://www.amazon.com /dp/B0881Z43R7

https://www.amazon.com /dp/B07VH3ZQD9

Contact Information: Jeff Hutchinson, jeffhutch@elearnlogic.com or (801) 376-6687.

Evaluation copy: http://www.elearnlogic.com/courseware.html

www.ingramcontent.com/pod-product-compliance
Lightning Source LLC
LaVergne TN
LVHW081758050326

832903LV00027B/2009